MARBLING

MARBLING

STUART SPENCER

Salem House
Topsfield, Massachusetts

First published in the United States by
Salem House Publishers, 1987,
462 Boston Street, Topsfield, MA 01983

Drawings by Pam Corfield

Printed and bound in Italy

ISBN: 0 88162 303 2

ACKNOWLEDGMENTS

The publishers would like to thank the following for allowing photographs to
be reproduced in this book: All paints by Dulux, page 74; Elizabeth
Whiting & Associates, pages 15, 27, 34, 38, 42 and 66; Michael Boys
Syndication, pages 43, 50, 55 and 63; Hand-painted units by Smallbone
Kitchens/Tiled splashback by Paris Ceramics, page 22.

CONTENTS

INTRODUCTION

The way in which we decorate our homes is as much a reflection of our character and personality as it is a measure of our practical skills and creative abilities. It is a form of expression in which we not only demonstrate our appreciation of line, form and colour, but also indicate our preference for atmosphere, mood and style.

While paint remains the quickest, easiest and cheapest way of colouring our environment, its versatility as a decorative tool has been hidden for many years beneath the shroud of functionalism, as mass production and standardization have played an ever increasing role in society.

Today, embellishment and ornamentation have become fashionable once more, and there has been a tremendous resurgence of interest in a whole range of craft-related subjects, none more popular or more accessible than that of the decorative paint techniques. Not only are the materials inexpensive and readily available over the retail counter, but the techniques are easily mastered by anyone who can wield a paint brush and follow simple instructions.

Fundamental to all techniques is the application of transparent colour in the form of a glaze to an opaque single-colour ground. While the paint is still wet or 'alive' it is moved or 'distressed' over the surface into the required pattern by using a selected distressing tool. Traditionally these are sponges, combs or cloths, etc. The tools and methods used give their names to these techniques, e.g., sponging, combing, ragging, dragging, etc. By using a combination of these techniques we are able to enter the area of illusion. The illusory paint techniques include antiquing, tortoiseshelling, woodgraining, bambooing, stencilling and, perhaps the most popular and widely applied of all, marbling.

The success of marbling as an illusory technique is based primarily on the simulation of the notable characteristics of the polished stone – those qualities of motion, depth, cloudiness and translucency which create a sense of cool mass and opulent serenity. By capturing these qualities in paint we are able to simulate polished marble.

The decorative potential of marble has been appreciated throughout recorded history; to this day it remains the most prestigious and atmospheric of building materials. It was formed when compressed beds of limestone rock containing all manner of mineral deposits and small inclusions such as pebbles, shells and fossils crystallized under the effects of great temperature and pressure. As the earth's crust buckled, tremendous forces caused stress fractures to occur. In time liquid debris leached into the resulting fissures and in solidifying produced the dramatic veining patterns so characteristic of many marbles. In extreme cases the bed shattered and angular fragments of marble were dispersed throughout the strata. Eventually they were randomly recombined in a cement of lime carbonate to produce the familiar brecciated marbles.

Once quarried, marble is cut into sections for ease of handling and positioning. These are polished to produce a highly reflective surface which is both functional and decorative. So diverse are the multifarious combinations of colour and pattern exhibited by the stone that the student of marbling need never be short of inspiration. To see marble in its true context, visit prestigious buildings such as museums or churches. It is only when viewed at this scale that many of the more dominant repeats appear and the true visual qualities of the stone become evident.

The technique of marbling attempts to capture the 'essence' of the polished stone in paint, either by the authentic replication of specific marbles or by a more casual representation of the qualities of the stone. There is evidence that this technique was first practised some 3,000 years ago, no doubt because then, as now, it provided a cost-effective alternative to the real thing.

1 PAINT, COLOUR AND GLAZES

PAINT TYPES

Paint is a versatile medium and is the most popular, practical and economic way of orchestrating colour within our environment. Water- and oil-based paints are the two major types available for common use within the field of decorative painting.

The price and quality of paint varies from one manufacturer to the next; always choose the best you can afford. Trade formulations are in particular far superior products to their retail counterparts. But avoid non-drip varieties as these are unsuitable for our purposes. Remember, oil- and water-based paints are incompatible and should not be mixed while in a fluid state.

Water-based paints

These are the popular emulsions. They are thinned with water, carry little smell and dry quickly. They are available in matt, mid sheen and gloss textures as emulsions, vinyl silk and vinyl enamel.

They can be applied with a brush or roller to all surfaces except bare metal which will rust. Hard gloss surfaces, however, must be thoroughly sanded and degreased before application to provide a key for the subsequent coats of paint.

Oil-based paints

These are thinned with white spirit, carry a pungent odour and are more expensive than their water-based counterparts. They, too are available in matt, mid sheen and gloss textures as undercoat, eggshell and gloss.

Undercoat and eggshell can be applied to any clean, dry surface with a brush or roller. When dry these surfaces may be sanded using glass paper or wet-and-dry paper to produce hard, flat, non-porous grounds suitable for the application of oil- or water-based paints. (Wet-and-dry paper is used with warm, soapy water to obtain a consistently abraded surface – the soap stops the paper from getting clogged.) Gloss grounds, however, should be avoided.

Tinting

Both water- and oil-based paints are available in a vast range of colours. But if a particular shade proves elusive most decorators shops offer a mixing scheme. Alternatively, you can make your own shades by adding tinters to the paint. For water-based paints use artists' acrylic or artists' gouache; for oil-based paints use artists' oils. Or Universal Tinters can be added to both types. These tinters contain excellent pigments and suitably thinned may be used as paint in their own right.

GLAZES AND WASHES

A glaze is the term applied to any oil- or water-based paint that has been thinned to obtain a degree of transparency, while a wash is the term applied to any oil- or water-based paint that has been so substantially

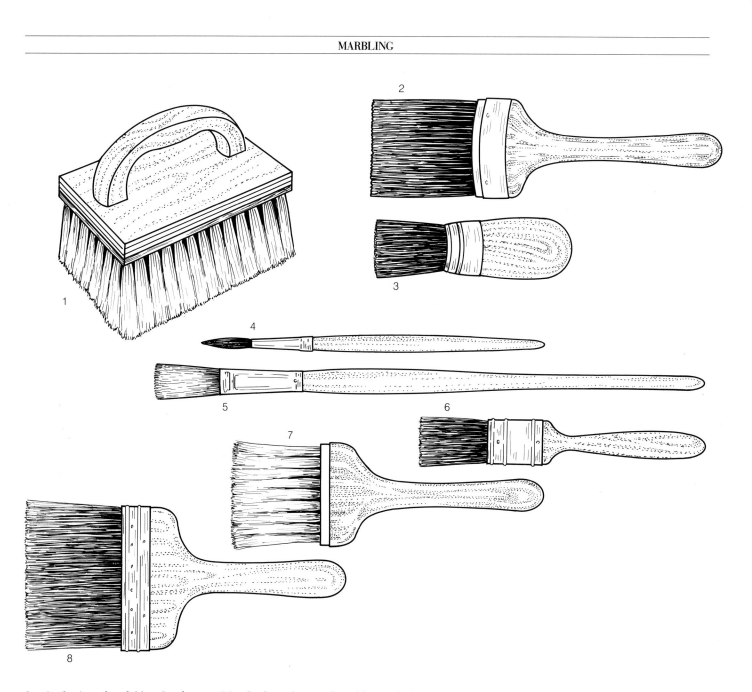

1 *A selection of useful brushes for practising broken colour and marbling techniques: 1 Stippling brush; 2 Hogs hair softener; 3 Stencil brush; 4 Artists' brush; 5 Fitch; 6, 7 and 8 Small, medium and large standard brushes*

A fantasy marble simulation featuring a busy veining pattern in delicate, softly stated colours has been applied to the walls and ceiling bringing character and warmth to this hallway.

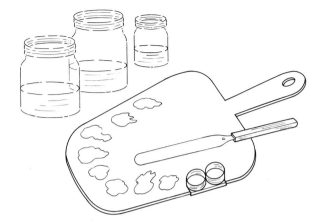

2 *For experimenting with colour combinations it will be useful to have the above: mixing jars for thinning glazes; a palette with clip on 'dippers' to keep different coloured paints in; and a palette knife*

thinned that it leaves merely a trace of colour on an opaque ground. In other words, a wash is just a well-thinned glaze.

In the field of decorative painting a glaze (or wash) is applied to an opaque, single colour ground. While the glaze is still wet or alive, its surface is moved into the required pattern. The time the glaze remains alive is critical and is a measure of the usefulness of the paint.

Water-based glazes dry very quickly which proves a fundamental drawback to more detailed work. The drying rate, however, can be affected by the following procedures:
1) Ensure the room in which you are working is cool and humid.
2) Do not overthin the glazes: the thinner the glaze the faster it will dry.
3) Add small quantities of glycerine to the glaze (a spoonful per litre).
4) Apply the glaze over a non-porous oil-based ground coat, i.e. undercoat or eggshell.

The rate at which oil-based glazes dry is more controllable than their water-based counterparts. They have, in consequence, a wider application in the field of decorative painting, and should be used where a detailed, authentic simulation of a marble type is required. The addition of linseed oil to the glaze will retard the drying time; adding liquid dryers will accelerate the process.

Water-based glaze
Method 1 Matt or mid sheen emulsion is thinned with water in the proportion of one part paint to approximately three parts water. The thinning ratio will depend on the strength of the pigment in the paint and the degree of transparency required.
Method 2 Pure artists' colours such as Universal Tinters, artists' acrylics or artists' gouache can be thinned with water to produce the required transparency. In general, the pigments are of excellent quality and the resulting glaze far more effective than the emulsion variety.

Water-based wash
Method 1 Matt emulsion is thinned with water in the proportion of one part paint to approximately eight parts water.
Method 2 Artists' colours, generally gouache, are thinned with water to the required transparency. A small amount of emulsion is sometimes added to give the paint a little 'body'.

When preparing water-based glazes and washes, artists' gouache can be used to tint the paint to the required colour.

Water-based glazes and washes may be applied to matt or mid sheen water-based paint, i.e. emulsion or vinyl silk, or matt or mid sheen oil-based paint i.e. undercoat or eggshell. Water-based washes however can only be used on matt emulsion. The slightest sheen causes the wash to 'ciss' – the paint coalesces into small droplets and runs off the surface.

Oil-based glaze

Method 1 Scumble glaze, a ready-made oil glaze, can be purchased from most paint suppliers. It is a transparent, viscous liquid which can be bought clear or tinted in matt, mid sheen or gloss textures. It is generally thinned, one part scumble glaze to one part white spirit.

Method 2 Thinned oil paint glaze. Undercoat or eggshell is mixed in the proportion of one part paint to approximately two parts white spirit, depending on the strength of the pigment and the degree of transparency required.

Method 3 Oil paint glaze. This is made by mixing one part undercoat with one part scumble glaze. The resulting mixture is then thinned with an equal quantity of white spirit.

Method 4 Home-made glaze. One part boiled linseed oil is mixed with two to three parts turpentine. A liquid dryer is then added to send the paint off. This mixture is sometimes referred to as a gilp.

Oil-based wash

Method 1 Undercoat or eggshell is thinned in the ratio of one part paint to eight parts white spirit. It is then tinted to the required shade using artists' oils.

Method 2 Artists' oils can be thinned with white spirit to achieve the required transparency.

Method 3 Scumble glaze, oil paint glaze or home-made glaze may also be used, thinned with white spirit and tinted with artists' oils.

In all cases artist oils can be used to tint the wash or glaze to the required shade.

PAINT AND COLOUR

We function in a world of colour, but while our response to colour is instinctive, our ability to articulate it is undoubtedly a skill.

Since leaving school it is unlikely that the majority of people will have picked up a paint brush with the idea of applying colour to a surface in an artistic manner. The most practical way of regaining confidence with colour is to invest in a basic set of artists' oil paints and water colours. They represent a microcosm of the colours, materials and techniques available to and used by both artist, craftsman and decorator alike. Artists' water-colours, such as acrylics or gouache, may be equated with the popular emulsions, while artists' oil paints find their equivalent in oil-based paints such as undercoat or eggshell. Practise combining colours on a palette to see what effects are possible.

To further investigate the formulation and interaction of colour, it is suggested that you refer to a *colour wheel*. The colour wheel is a visual chart that illustrates the established principles of the structure of colour. The three *primary colours* or hues are red, yellow and blue. In theory they are pure colour that cannot be made by mixing other colours. The *secondary colours* are produced by mixing two primaries, for example mix yellow and red to get orange. The *tertiary colours* are produced by mixing a primary and a secondary. *Tints* are produced by adding white to a colour, while *shades* are produced by adding black, although *tone* is a more commonly used word to describe the lightness or darkness of a colour. *Complementary colours* are the colours which are directly opposite each other on the colour wheel. These colours when placed side by side heighten each other's purity; when mixed in equal quantities they cancel each other out and produce grey. To tone a colour down whilst retaining its purity it is necessary to use its exact complement. In practice

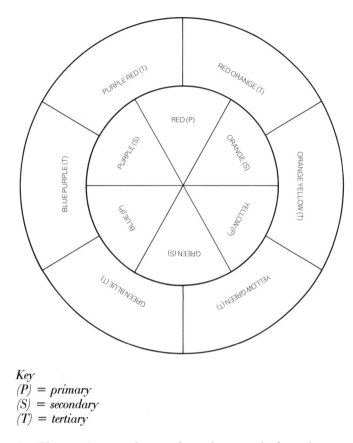

Key
(P) = primary
(S) = secondary
(T) = tertiary

3 *When a primary and a secondary colour are mixed a tertiary colour is produced*

however we use the earth colours to take the heat out of a hue. The *earth colours* are used extensively throughout the decorative paint techniques. They are raw umber, a brown red-purple; burnt umber, a deep brown red-

purple; raw sienna, a light yellow-brown red-purple; burnt sienna, a deep brown red-red purple; French yellow ochre, a yellow red-purple; and lamp black, a black blue. To tone a colour down use an earth colour that contains the complementary of that colour. The earth colours are gentle and subdued and are popularly used within marbling to create subtle understated tones.

Although in theory all colours can be created by intermixing the primaries, in practice a vast range of colours are readily available in tubes from art shops in both oil- and water-based paints.

COLOUR AND TRANSPARENCY

In the field of the decorative paint techniques the most important feature exhibited by paint is its ability to retain the vitality and intensity of colour even when thinned to transparency. When we use paint in a conventional manner, we choose an off-the-shelf colour, thin and apply according to the manufacturers' instructions. The object is to achieve a flat, even cover of paint which effectively obscures the background. Opacity is the key word. This is known as a single or flat colour technique.

If we take the same pot of paint and thin more than is recommended, we sacrifice the opacity. Further thinning will result in the paint becoming transparent. In this state it is known as a glaze. The fact that it reveals an underlying colour is regarded as a positive advantage. We actually see colour through colour. Transparency is the key word. When we articulate glazes on an opaque ground we enter the world of the broken colour techniques.

2 THE TECHNIQUES

BROKEN COLOUR TECHNIQUES

The decorative potential of the broken colour techniques is based on the endless subtleties produced when a broken film of paint in the form of a glaze is contrasted against an opaque ground coat. This broken film can be achieved in two ways by the additive or the subtractive method.

With the additive method a coloured opaque ground coat is applied to a prepared surface. A glaze is then made in a contrasting colour. Then, using a selected distressing tool, a sponge or cloth for example, the glaze is systematically dabbed onto the surface.

Using the subtractive method the glaze is evenly

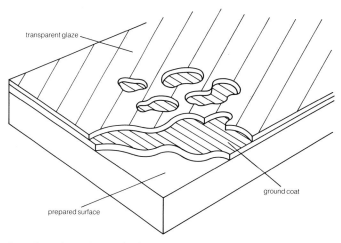

5 *The subtractive method*

applied with a brush to the entire surface. Then, while still wet, the surface is systematically distressed by dabbing the wet glaze with a brush, a dry cloth or a sponge. In this way, flecks of glaze are removed from the surfaces revealing the ground.

In both cases, when used over large areas the object is to achieve a random pattern of uniform density.

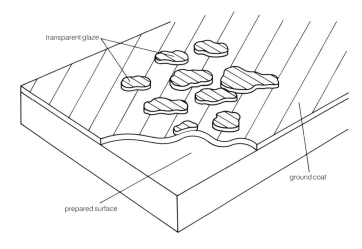

4 *The additive method*

Sponging

This can be an additive or a subtractive technique. In each case a tight speckled finish is produced by distressing the glaze with a sponge. Use natural marine sponges rather than the artificial variety. Although more expensive, they produce a print which is less insistent and regimented.

Sponging on (or sponge stipple) Prepare the ground (page 33). Place a prepared coloured glaze in a sloping tray. Take up a small amount of glaze on the sponge and test the print on paper before applying it to the surface. Apply the glaze systematically to the surface with a light dabbing action.

7 *Once the first glaze has dried, a second coloured glaze can be applied to give a marbled effect*

6 *Sponging on: apply the glaze with a light dabbing action to create a soft, cloudy effect*

Sponging off Prepare the ground (page 33). Apply a prepared coloured glaze to the surface with a brush. While the glaze is alive, dab the surface with a clean dry sponge. Flecks of glaze are removed from the surface to reveal the underlying ground colour. Attempt to expose approximately half the ground coat. When working these techniques you should vary the wrist action and readjust your hold on the sponge to prevent mechanical repetition of the print. Over large areas try for a random pattern of uniform density. Every so often the sponge should be rung out in a solvent to avoid a build up of glaze which would produce a smudged print. When the applied glaze has dried, repeat the process using a glaze of a contrasting colour.

Ragging

This can be an additive or subtractive technique. The distressing tool is any piece of cloth that is colour fast, clean and lint free. It can be used as a loosely gathered-up ball to dab the surface (ragging on/off), or rolled into a sausage shape and rolled over the surface (rag rolling on/off). The finish can be varied from a subdued clouded effect to a dramatic textured effect.

Rag/rag rolling on Prepare the ground (page 33). Place the prepared glaze in a sloping tray. Form the cloth into the required shape and dip into the glaze. Remove excess glaze and test the print on paper before applying to the surface. Work methodically using the dabbing or rolling motion.

Rag/rag rolling off Prepare the ground (page 33). Apply the glaze to the surface using a brush. Distress the glaze while alive with a clean dry cloth using a dabbing or rolling technique.

Discard the cloths when they become charged with glaze. Varying the distressing action and reforming the cloth will avoid mechanical repetition. Overlays of different coloured glazes can be applied when underlying glazes have dried.

9   *Ragging off produces more subtle prints implying cloudiness and depth*

8   *The dramatic effects achieved by rag rolling on imply motion and depth*

Combing

Combing is a subtractive technique. It can produce a variety of effects from the subtleties associated with

The central panels of these kitchen units have been sponged to give a marble-like finish. They are framed by dragged borders.

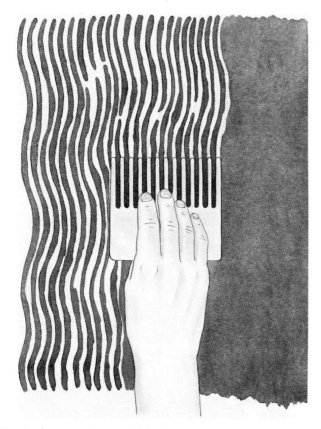

10 *Combing produces a bold, obvious pattern. The pattern will, of course, be greatly affected by the size of the comb's teeth.*

11 *Compared to combing, the technique of dragging produces a much finer effect*

woodgraining to the bold patterns of floor design.

Although combs can be bought from most decorating shops, a great deal of flexibility and variation can be achieved by making your own from any semi-rigid material.

Prepare the ground (page 33). Apply the coloured glaze with a brush in a continuous film to the surface. Run the comb through the wet glaze to produce the required pattern.

Dragging

Although any type of brush can be used, a specialist brush produces a subtle finish which avoids the regimented pin striping effect produced by ordinary brushes. The technique is much used in woodgraining.

Prepare the ground (page 33). Apply the coloured

glaze with a brush in a continuous film over the surface. While the glaze is still alive, pull the dragging brush through the glaze in a continuous downward motion. Work systematically over the surface, as the effect relies on the consistency of the technique. Diagonal overlapping strokes can be introduced to produce a variety of effects.

Glaze is picked off the surface onto the bristles of the brush revealing the ground colour, and the brush must be cleaned at regular intervals to prevent smearing in the glaze.

12 *Spattering: take up the glaze on a stiff-bristled brush (a stencil brush is ideal) and run your thumb over the bristles to scatter droplets onto the surface. This will produce a multicoloured pattern of tiny pinheads of glaze, simulating the surface of granites and porphyries.*

Spattering

Spattering is an additive technique. It produces a multicoloured pattern of tiny pin heads of glaze scattered randomly over the surface. It is used extensively in simulating the surface of granites and porphyries.

Prepare the ground (page 33). Take up the glaze on a stiff-bristled brush and scatter droplets onto the surface. The droplets may be released by either striking the shaft of the brush on a hard surface, such as a ruler, or running a finger over the bristles.

A variation is to fire the glaze at the surface in a thin stream. The glaze is poured into the finger of a rubber glove; a hole is pierced in the end, and the finger is squeezed to release the glaze onto the surface. This can produce dramatic results, but is rather uncontrollable.

Another variation is a technique known as cissing. The brush is charged with solvent and the spattering procedure repeated. Small droplets are released onto the surface causing recently applied paint to ciss. The glaze opens and colours merge and blend. It is widely used in the marbling technique to produce the effects of cloudiness and depth. Spattering is best operated on a horizontal surface as thinned paint tends to run off vertical surfaces.

Stippling

Stippling is a subtractive technique which can disguise brush marks, and produces interesting shading effects. For large areas a stippling brush is required. For small areas any stiff-bristled, flat-headed brush will do.

Prepare the ground (page 33). Apply the glaze with a brush in a continuous film to the surface. While the glaze is still wet, the surface is struck rhythmically with the flat head of the stippling brush, and small flecks of glaze are removed to reveal the ground colour. The bristles of the brush should be cleaned at regular intervals to prevent smudging.

13 *Stippling: apply the glaze to the surface; while the glaze is still wet strike the surface rhythmically with a flat-headed brush removing small flecks of glaze to reveal the ground coat. For large areas use a stippling brush; for small areas any stiff-bristled, flat-headed brush will do, such as a dusting brush or even a broom (particularly useful for stippling ceilings).*

MARBLING TECHNIQUES

Now the techniques which have specific application to marbling can be described. Mastery of these techniques will allow you to adopt a confident, systematic approach to simulating real or fantasy marbles. By using these techniques individually or collectively the characteristic effects of the natural stone can be captured.

Veining

Veining is the most dramatic visual characteristic of marble but to capture the elusive meandering qualities of the veining patterns, success depends to a great extent on understanding the way veins were formed.

Veins are the visible evidence of the forces that acted on the stone deep within the earth's crust, causing it to melt and fracture. Forces have a source, a strength and a direction and the veins may be likened to the patterns produced when a pane of glass or a mirror is broken. Although the radiating lines are random, this pattern has a coherent meaning. Thus, when marbling, while veins may cross and recross the ground, they should never

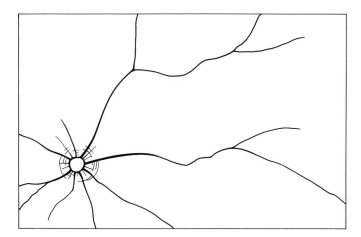

14 *The fracture lines on a shattered mirror provide a good reference for drawing a veining pattern*

make a sudden appearance in the middle of your work. If they do, they read as a visual nonsense.

Veining patterns do not all lie in the same plane as the surface of the marble. While some may lay just beneath the surface, in some cases actually breaking the surface, others recede into the depths and dissolve beneath shadowy veils. This feature is partially responsible for the feeling of mystery that emanates from the stone.

When creating veining patterns, wherever possible consult the natural stone. Photographs, slides and tracings will prove invaluable when an exact simulation is required. Or, alternatively, examine the patterns formed by a fractured pane of glass, a branching twig, or a torn net curtain. Notice how sometimes these veining patterns follow parallel lines or courses, whilst other times they intersect, either overlapping or colliding and intermingling.

Veining patterns project great strength of line. In order not to overstate the element they must be represented in softly muted colour.

Oil-based paints provide us with an excellent medium in which to capture the subtleties of the veining patterns. The technique of softening and blending (page 31) allows the strength of line, density of colour and apparent depth of the vein beneath the surface to be accurately controlled – by accentuating parts of the vein we cause it to advance, by softening we cause it to retreat into the background colour.

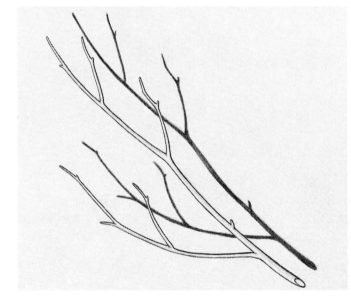

15 *Place a branching twig on a piece of white paper, and backlight (with a torch for example) to throw its shadow onto the paper. Trace off the shadow for an effective veining pattern.*

16 *An artists' brush is used to paint the main veins onto the marbled surface. Hold the brush well up the shaft and apply the paint with an unsteady, shaking, fidgeting motion.*

In this room, the decorative paint techniques of marbling and gilding have been combined to create a classical theme.

Water-based paints, however, are difficult to blend and produce a far less convincing result. The veins tend to sit only in the plane of the marbled surface. However these paints may be suitable for working on a larger area where an accurate representation of the stone is not required.

The veining patterns can be produced by using a variety of tools:

Brushes To produce the indefinite meandering qualities of a vein tease the paint onto the surface using an artists' brush or flat fitch. The brush is held well up the shaft and the paint is applied with an unsteady shaking hand, a fidgeting motion. Rolling the tip of the brush and varying the pressure will ensure that at one moment the head of the brush is fanned, at the next it is drawn into a fine point. Occasionally lift the brush from the surface, but rejoin it an instant later to establish continuity.

Goose feather Soak the flight to break the fronds up into smaller elements which can be regarded as individual brush heads. The feather is first dipped in solvent and then in the glaze. The feather may be turned, twisted or angled in any number of ways to produce any number of veining patterns, from wide sweeping parallel bands to tiny, delicate intersecting networks.

Coloured crayons may be used in both the oil and water based methods and provide us with a speed and

17 *A goose feather with its fronds broken up to create individual brush heads provides a useful tool for producing a wide variety of veining patterns*

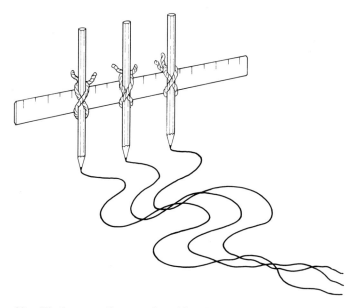

18 *Tie three pencils to a ruler with string and elastic bands. Pull the ruler across the surface, twisting and turning as you go to create an interesting veining pattern.*

delicacy of technique which is not easily obtainable in paint. Oil-based crayons may be applied to a dry surface or a wet glaze. If applied to a wet glaze they may be softened and blended within the medium with a hogs hair softening brush. For the water-based method, use coloured pencils on a dry surface. Brands, however, should be tested before use for their compatibility with the varnish coat.

Cottons or twine may be used individually, or collectively in the form of a tassle, to add or subtract paint from the surface. Either dip the threads into glaze and lay them on the prepared ground, or lay them onto a wet glaze and dab them with a flat object so they take up or displace the glaze. This will produce fine sketchy lines which can be superimposed on more dominant patterns without reducing their effectiveness.

Newspaper Lay a sheet of creased newspaper onto a wet glazed surface, and dab or move with a brush. The glaze is either displaced or absorbed by the paper to reveal the underlying ground. This technique is known as paper rocking.

When a veining pattern has been established, opaque paint can be applied with an artists' brush to give emphasis to certain areas by lightening or darkening. This technique helps to define how close to the surface of the stone the vein lies.

Cissing

Cissing is a general technique used throughout decorative painting, and it is widely used in marbling to produce the qualities of cloudiness and depth.

The oil-based method White spirit, the solvent for the oil-based method, is applied to the wet surface of the glaze in several ways to create different effects.

Method 1 Release the solvent onto the wet glaze in droplets by spattering with a stencil brush or similar. This will cause the glaze to form rings or pools.

19 *Cissing: apply a glaze to the entire surface. Dip a stencil brush in solvent and strike the shaft of the brush onto the edge of a ruler to release droplets onto the still wet glaze.*

Method 2 Dab the surface of the glaze with a stippling action using a brush carrying the solvent, or load an artists' brush with solvent and pull through the glaze to cause a line to open up.

Method 3 Dab the surface of the glaze with a screwed up cloth or paper which has been moistened with the solvent, to produce fine intersecting lines and angular shapes.

In each case the object is to reveal the ground colour by dispersing the glaze (this is known as opening up the glaze), and to soften, blend and cloud the coloured glazes into one another forming subtle hues.

The action of the solvent can be controlled by mopping up any excesses with a tissue or cotton wool. This must be done carefully to avoid removing paint from the surface.

Where large amounts of solvent are to be introduced, cissing is best carried out on a horizontal surface. If a vertical surface is used, the glaze will run into troughs and the colour will concentrate at the bottom of these. However, if this effect is controlled it can produce attractive cloudy features with gently accented boundaries.

As an alternative to white spirit, use turpentine as the solvent for the oil-based method to produce slightly accentuated effects.

The water-based method Water is the solvent for the water-based paints. Use any of the three methods described above. However, be aware that due to the nature of the medium, cissing is far less effective on water-based paints. The technique should only be carried out on a horizontal surface.

Wiping out
With this technique the wet glaze is removed from or displaced on the surface to reveal the ground colour. This can be done in a number of ways.

Method 1 A clean cloth used either dry or moistened with solvent is wrapped around the forefinger and used to remove the glaze from the required section.

Method 2 The glaze is displaced by a pencil rubber or cork or similar object.

Method 3 Run a wooden stick through the glaze to create a line. An angled end produces a line which can be varied from thin to thick.

This technique is very flexible. It can be used to remove unwanted elements or mistakes from the marbled work, and to achieve greater translucency in subsequently applied glazes by allowing light to be

20 *Wiping out: here a piece of cork cut lengthways is used to displace the wet glaze to reveal the ground coat*

reflected through from the white ground. It is also used specifically in the simulation of the brecciated and fossiliferous marbles. For brecciated marbles it is used to identify angular fragments of rock. To create fossiliferous marbles, all sorts of printing elements are used to simulate the skeletons of fossils trapped in the limestone rock. These range from sliced vegetables to balloons.

Although this technique is applicable to both the oil- and water-based methods, it is not recommended where water-based glazes have been applied over emulsion ground coats: the applied water-based glazes soften the ground and this technique may cause smudging.

Isolating
Isolating is a technique used to protect a delicate surface

midway through a marble simulation by applying a thin protective layer of transparent varnish. The varnish acts not only as a protective layer but also as a window through which the coloured ground may be seen. Thus superimposed glazes may be wiped out to reveal the delicate backdrop without fear of damaging the surface. The technique is used specifically to protect water-based grounds from applied water-based or oil-based glazes.

The varnish, which may be the quick-drying white polish or the slow drying matt or mid sheen polyurethane varnish, must be applied to a dry surface. When the varnish has dried it should be lightly abraded with fine (800s) wet-and-dry paper using warm soapy water. This will provide a key for subsequent glazes. The surface must be thoroughly dried before the application of more paint. Water-based glazes may be combined with fullers earth, a 'fixing' agent available from art shops, to prevent the glaze from 'cissing up' or gathering.

Softening and blending
When you look into the surface of marble clearly defined elements can be identified, such as veins, pebbles and fossils. As they recede from the surface their outlines blur and fade, and their colour softens and becomes muted. Deeper within the stone they dissolve into a mottled ground of soft veils and imprecise shadows. This characteristic, which is known as cloudiness, is primarily responsible for the qualities of mystery and depth that we find in many marbles. The technique of softening and blending is used to simulate the dissolving of line and the subtle transition of colour and tone found in marble. When this process is applied to the entire surface it is known as 'scumbling' or 'clouding' the ground to provide a backdrop on which to construct details such as veins.

Water-based paints are completely unsuitable for this technique as the paint dries too quickly leaving insuf-ficient time to recreate the controlled gradation of line and colour. The medium itself is so insubstantial that it is difficult to induce suspended coloured pigments to flow and intermingle. And it is this inability to soften and blend water-based paints that marks the split between serious marbling and casual stylization.

Because of the greater degree of control that it is possible to exert over the medium, the oil-based method provides an excellent opportunity to develop and exploit the subtleties of softening and blending.

Before softening and blending a thin coat of scumble glaze must be applied to the prepared ground. This is called 'oiling-in' the ground. This glaze may be regarded as a moisturizing layer on which applied colour may be floated, moved, softened and blended. The glaze will stay alive or workable for several minutes.

21 *A hogs hair softener is used to soften and blend in all directions*

Paint Two selected artists' oil colours, say yellow ochre and burnt sienna, scumble glaze, white spirit.

Equipment Artists' palette board, two 25 mm (1 in) flat brushes, two dippers containing the medium and white spirit, two containers, hogs hair softener.

Method The technique will be worked on an eggshell ground (page 33).

Individually blend the colours on the palette with white spirit, and create two transparent glazes in the containers.

Thin the scumble glaze with a little white spirit. Using a cloth or brush 'oil-in' the ground by applying a continuous layer of the thinned scumble glaze to the panel.

Take up one of the coloured glazes and apply it to the oiled ground in random irregular patches and squiggles. Repeat the procedure using the other glaze. To get a further degree of transparency to the glaze occasionally dip the brush in white spirit, scumble glaze and then the coloured glaze. The whole of the ground should be more or less covered with the applied glazes.

Blend and soften the colours in all directions using the hogs hair softener. Hold the brush loosely in the hand, applying just sufficient pressure to make the bristles flex. If areas of the panel require strengthening, apply more glaze and repeat the blending procedure.

Introduce features such as veining patterns (pages 25–29) onto the scumbled ground while the medium is still pliable so they can be softened and blended.

Over a period of a few hours the ground will become tacky and harden off. Attempts to carry out further softening will result in the glaze smearing.

Wash the brush out in white spirit and clean with soapy water. Hang to dry.

3 GETTING STARTED

PRACTISING THE TECHNIQUES

Before attempting to reproduce any specific marble types, it is recommended that some time be spent trying out the broken colour and marbling techniques described in the last chapter. Work systematically through these techniques to see just what kind of effects can be achieved.

Time spent experimenting now will prove invaluable later on. As this is very much an experimental stage, it is a good idea to use a surface that can be easily washed off such as melamine or Formica. Alternatively, use Fablon, a thin plastic, adhesive film, available in a range of colours from DIY shops. If Fablon is used, off-cuts may be kept to record results for future reference, guidance and inspiration.

Once you have confidently mastered these basic techniques you are ready to begin reproducing specific marble types. Whether you attempt a casual stylization or an authentic replication of a marble the basic sequence remains the same.

THE BASIC SEQUENCE

This involves preparation of the surface, preparation of the ground, marbling the ground, varnishing the marbling, and polishing the varnish.

Preparation of the surface

The surface of polished marble is perfectly flat and smooth. The surface on which we intend to construct our technique should be free of nibbs and ripples. Remember, paint can do nothing to rectify irregularities in the surface. (See Chapter 7 for advice on preparing specific surfaces.) Diligent preparation is always reflected in the finish.

Preparation of the ground

The purpose of the ground is to provide a smooth, hard, non-absorbent surface on which to marble. It also provides a reflective surface which produces the element of translucency evident in all the pale coloured marbles. For a general all-purpose ground suitable for both the oil- and water-based methods. apply two full strength coats of white undercoat to the prepared surface allowing sufficient time for drying between each coat. Leave overnight to harden off. Lightly dry sand with fine (220s grade) glass paper. Apply two full strength coats of trade eggshell allowing sufficient time for drying between each coat. Leave to harden for two days. Abrade the surface with fine-medium wet-and-dry (600s grade) paper using warm soapy water and a flat rubbing block. Wipe the surface and allow it to stand and dry out.

Marbling the ground

See Chapters 4 and 5 for specific instructions on creating a wide variety of marble types using water- and oil-based paints.

Almost every surface in this room has been treated with a fantasy variegated marble simulation: the strategic positioning of mirrors helps to open up the room and prevents the effect from becoming overbearing.

Varnishing

Varnish is applied to the marbled surface to protect it and to give a decorative finish.

Protection Varnish is a transparent film of paint which drys to a smooth hard finish. It may be necessary to apply several coats: for example for a wall surface one or two coats will be adequate, whereas a heavily-used floor may need as many as six coats to ensure full protection.

Decoration Marble exhibits a variety of surface finishes ranging from a dull lustre to a highly reflective glassy sheen. Varnishes provide all the necessary textures and are available in matt, mid sheen and gloss finishes. Special effects can be produced by intermixing the different textures, for example, applying a matt or mid sheen varnish over a dry coat of gloss varnish produces an effect that relieves the harshness of the gloss finish but still retains the deep lustre.

Polyurethane varnish is a moden oil-based varnish which is suitable for application to either an oil- or a water-based marbling technique. Rubbing down between coats can provide very flat reflective surfaces: Use medium to ultrafine grade wet-and-dry paper (600s to 1200s grit). Gloss surfaces are difficult to sand unless they are well cured. Ensure that the surface is perfectly dry before applying more varnish.

White polish made from bleached shellac is a varnish which dries almost immediately it is applied to a surface. Although it does not provide a strong film, many coats can be built up in a short period of time. It can be used to level out any relief that may have resulted from a build up of glazes and it is easy to wet and dry to a smooth flat surface. Over this the more durable polyurethane varnish can be applied as a protective top coat. White polish should only be bought in small quantities as it tends to become unworkable once it has been exposed to air.

Polishing

Where quality flat, highly reflective surfaces are required, for example on table tops, it is necessary to polish the varnished surface. Abrade the varnished surface with very fine (1000s) wet-and-dry paper. Use plenty of warm soapy water to avoid clogging of the paper. If the surface of the technique has been carried out on an extremely flat surface a rubbing block may be used; if not the wet-and-dry paper must be held in the palm of the hand. Use a circular motion and change the paper regularly.

Products readily available from car accessory shops provide ideal polishing materials. Rubbing compound paste comes in several grades. The coarsest can be very abrasive. Take care not to rub through the varnish, however, and spoil the technique. Place on a soft cloth and apply with a circular rubbing action. For an even higher gloss, use a liquid polisher. Repeat the process above finishing off with a clean dry cloth. Finish with a domestic aerosol wax.

MARBLED PANELS

Traditionally when used as a decorative veneer marble is cut into rectilinear panels to ease the positioning of the stone onto wall or floor areas. By marking out large surfaces into panels and designing each individually we bring an immediate authenticity and authority to our work. The panelling system has other advantages too. In particular it enables large surfaces to be marbled more easily by breaking the area up into manageable sections.

Carefully composed panels, thoughtfully positioned, with pronounced horizontal or vertical accents can greatly alter the proportions of an interior. Ceilings can be visually raised or lowered, walls can be distanced or drawn in (figs. 22–5, page 36). Panels can be worked over a large area to create a subtle back-drop in a room, or the shape of panels can be emphasized to make a

The following diagrams show how carefully composed and well-positioned panels can affect the visual proportions of a room

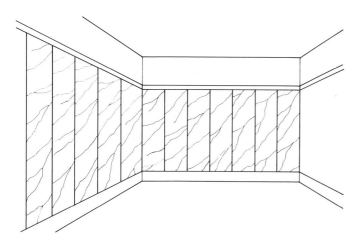

22 *Marbled panels constructed from skirting board to picture rail with a strong vertical accent helps to visually raise the ceiling*

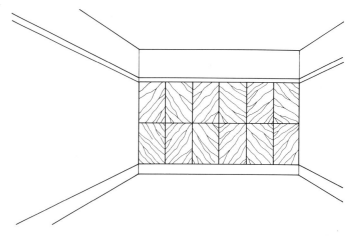

23 *Marbled panels from skirting board to picture rail with alternating diagonal accents can help to draw in a large room*

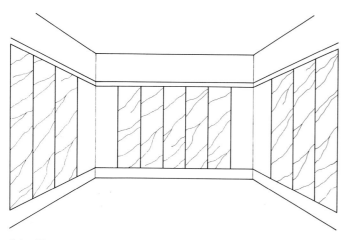

24 *To space out a small room, do not extend the marbled panels into the corners. Again, construct the panels from skirting board to picture rail to visually raise the ceiling level.*

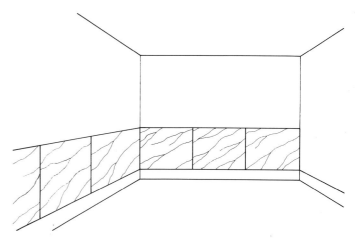

25 *A high ceiling can be made visually lower by emphasizing the horizontal accents in the room. Construct the marbled panels up to dado height.*

feature by contrasting them against flat painted surfaces or alternatively by outlining them with a contrasting marbled border.

These panels can be marked out directly onto the surface to be marbled or onto large sheets of hardboard. It is advised that you first attempt simulating the marbles described in Chapters 4 and 5 onto a small panel 60 cm × 90 cm (2 ft × 3 ft). At this stage it may be an idea to work onto a white, washable plastic surface, such as melamine or Fablon.

Composing a panel

The disposition of line, form and colour within each panel must be planned to achieve a balanced harmonious composition. Before beginning to sketch out a design, refer wherever possible to the natural polished stone. Prepare a series of sketches bearing in mind the following points:

Proportion This is the way lines, shapes and colours relate to one another, to the panel as a whole, and to other panels within an overall design.

Veining patterns are often the strongest feature in the design. Diagonals imply movement and can be used to divide panels into visually pleasing areas. Intersecting horizontals and verticals tend to be solid, uninspired and should be avoided. An exception to this is black and gold marble whose veining pattern is always depicted as a strong vertical accent. Veining patterns should as a general rule relate to the major areas of colour on your panel so that the two elements are linked.

Colours Remember, if a panel is used in a vertical position the weight of colour should be concentrated in the bottom half of the panel. If it is placed in the top, the panel becomes top heavy and unbalanced.

As far as choosing colours is concerned, this is a personal choice but do remember that light colours are optimistic and expansive and can open up a small room,

whereas large cavernous rooms can be drawn in by using bold, warm, earth colours.

Translucency is a feature exhibited by many marbles. It is characterized by what appears to be an inner light shining from within the stone. Veils of colour and shadowy veining features float imprecisely within the light producing a feeling of depth and mystery. Try to capture these qualities in your design by using well thinned transparent glazes which allow the white eggshell ground to reflect light through the applied paint. The indeterminate quality of the surface suggests space and provides a useful illusion to relieve cramped or claustrophobic environments.

When you are satisfied with a sketched design get a feel for the scale of your simulation by transferring the major features onto your panel in chalk.

Identify colours that you wish to use. Select the required tinters, arrange them in tonal value around the palette and mix the required colour. If necessary make notes of this recipe. These are good for future reference. Prepare glazes and paint out a small panel to test colour relationships and proportion by defining the prominent areas of colour.

When you are happy with the results you are ready to begin applying a selected marbling technique to the panel.

GOOD WORKING HABITS
In order to obtain a successful painted finish certain ground rules must be followed.

Paint

Let the materials stand at room temperature for at least a day. Wipe the containers and blow dust off the lid before opening. Follow manufacturer's instructions for stirring and thinning. Strain the paint through a filter into a clean pot to remove undissolved lumps.

The wall surface has been divided into panels, framed by borders; both have been marbled using the same softly stated colours, but using a slight variation in the pattern. The overall effect is to give life and movement to a large wall area.

Brushes

Separate brushes should be used for oil- and water-based paints. Varnishing brushes should be used for the purpose of varnishing alone.

Before using a varnishing brush, charge the bristles with varnish and work the brush. This will eliminate frothing and milkiness when varnish is applied to the surface. Discard the charging material.

After use, brushes should be cleaned with their respective solvents (water or white spirit), washed in detergent, rinsed in clean water and hung up to dry.

Surface

The surface should be at room temperature. If possible raise the surface off the floor onto a clean work area.

Before applying paint make sure the surface is completely free of dust.

The room

Clean the room, allow the dust to settle and provide sufficient ventilation. Keep the temperature as constant as possible. Avoid cold damp draughts; they will cause the surface to bloom (go milky). Keep the air as still as possible.

Applying the paint

Provide full even coats without misses, scuffs or brush marks. Apply quickly and maintain a wet edge. Don't return to previously painted areas. Wear suitable protective clothing.

4 MARBLING WITH WATER-BASED PAINTS

Marbling with the quick-drying water-based paints is for those who require a speedy, cheap, cheerful result. Although finishes can never pretend to anything more than casual stylisations, their compelling visual features provide us with a useful method of establishing character in anonymous areas such as halls, landings, cloakrooms and corridors; disguising surface imperfections (use matt paint); relieving unfortunate proportions; and camouflaging eyesores such as pipes and radiators.

Water-based finishes relate more to the grand effect and marbling should be applied in an uninhibited relaxed manner. Concentrate more on colour than detail; be dramatic rather than subtle.

The speed at which water-based paints dry provides an ideal opportunity to investigate colour relationships and try out the broken colour and marbling techniques described in Chapter 2. With thin glazes drying in a matter of seconds, it is possible in the space of an afternoon to come to grips with the basics of marbling.

Because we are very much at an experimental stage it is a good idea to marble onto a surface that may be washed off, such as melamine or a white, plastic film like Fablon.

As a starting point for all the marble types described in this chapter it is recommended that the ground coat described on p. 33 be applied to the surface, although any matt or mid sheen oil- or water-based paint would be suitable.

PORPHYRY

Although porphyry is not strictly speaking a marble, it has been prized as a decorative stone for thousands of years. Porphyry is in fact the collective name applied to a group of igneous rocks whose polished surface exhibits a uniform density of tiny increments of contrasting colours within a predominant colour which is usually reddy-purple, but greys, greens, violets and browns are also found.

Small flecks of semi-transparent colour are applied to a prepared ground by sponging or spattering. The paint dries rapidly and glazes may be applied one over the other in quick succession. The simulation of fantasy porphyries thus provides an excellent opportunity to investigate colour relationships. Where large areas are tackled the ground must be pale and the applied glazes bright and sparingly applied, e.g. primary colours over cream. For smaller areas the colours can be more dense and dramatic, such as gold over black, or purple over red.

The sponging technique

This method is preferred by those who require an authentic simulation of the rock as greater control can be exercised over the size, disposition and transparency of the coloured flecks.

Paint A selection of gouache colours is advisable. These may be used as colours in their own right, or to tint thinned white emulsion. Choose strong colours that range from light to dark to give depth to the composition, and apply over a white eggshell ground to ensure a translucent effect.

Equipment A marine sponge.

Method Prepare four transparent glazes from the selected colours.

Dip the sponge in the darkest colour, test the print on paper, and apply sparingly to the ground in a dabbing manner. This is known as sponge stippling. Aim to cover the surface with a uniform density. Wait for each layer of glaze to dry before applying another.

Repeat the procedure using progressively lighter tones of glaze. The last colour applied should be the predominant colour of the simulation.

Finally, seal and protect the surface with varnish.

The spattering technique

Paint As above.

Equipment Long-handled stencil brush.

Method Prepare four transparent glazes from the selected colours and beginning with the darkest colour, take up the glaze on the stencil brush and release the colour onto the surface by striking the shaft of the brush on a ruler.

Repeat this procedure using the progressively lighter tones of glaze. Remember to wait for each glaze to dry before applying subsequent glazes. Seal the finish with varnish.

Alternative technique

To create a textured back-drop on which to work, apply a coloured glaze to the ground and distress by pulling a dragging brush or fine comb through it. The print should be delicate and cross-hatched, and subsequently applied glazes sufficiently transparent to reveal a glimpse of the patterning beneath.

BRECCIATED MARBLE

After marble has formed, deep within the earth's crust, it is often subjected to tremendous forces which shatter the beds into angular fragments. These fragments are eventually cemented back together to produce marble that when cut and polished exhibits a pattern like crazy paving.

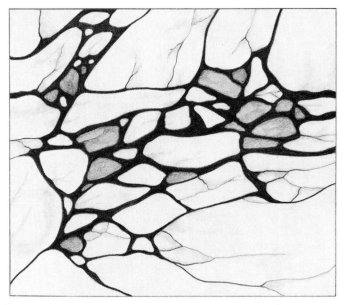

26 *Brecciated marble*

Paint Black, white, Indian red, ultramarine, lake, ochre. Glycerine.

Equipment Cloth, stippler, artificial sponge cut into angular fragments, artists' brush.

Method 1 Prepare a blue-grey glaze from white, ultramine, blue and black. Add a few drops of glycerine to extend the drying time, thin to transparency and apply to the prepared ground with a cloth. The glaze should leave only sufficient colour on the surface to dirty the ground.

A casual stylization of a Sienna marble has been extensively used on the walls of this living room in a colour which complements the real fossilized marble interior of the fireplace.

The entrance columns to this elegant dining room have been finished with a white veined marble simulation to help to establish an authentic classical look.

While the glaze is alive, wipe out the areas where the angular sections are due to be printed. This will ensure that the superimposed transparent coloured glazes will appear fresh and translucent. Allow the glaze to dry.

Prepare glazes of grey violet, deep red and purple by blending Indian red, ultramarine, lake and black. Thin the glazes to transparency. Take up the glazes on the angular sections of sponge and print them on the wiped out sections leaving a margin of the ground showing through between them.

Using an artists' brush outline the veining pattern in translucent glazes ranging in colour from red to light grey. Enclose some of the blue-grey ground in the veining pattern. Detail accents in opaque colour.

Seal the finish with polyurethane varnish.

Method 2 To the prepared ground rag-on glazes of grey-violet, deep-red and purple in patches, leaving about a quarter of the ground uncovered. Texture some sections of the glaze by sponge stippling.

Isolate the surface with a coat of mid-sheen polyurethane varnish. Allow to dry.

Prepare glazes of grey-purple and white. Rag them over the entire ground in irregular overlapping patches.

Using a cork or an eraser, wipe out angular sections to reveal the ground. This displaced paint will indicate the veining pattern. Strengthen features in the veining pattern and in the ground by using opaque colour. Again, seal the finish with polyurethane varnish.

VARIEGATED MARBLES

These dramatic marbles exhibit cloudy veiled backgrounds and sinewy veining patterns. When simulating this marble the ground is worked first, and then the veining patterns are superimposed onto it. Therefore, to make sense of the composition it is desirable to visually link the two by using the ground colour formations, to indicate the veining pattern: for example, by drawing the line of a vein around a cloudy detail or squeezing a vein between shaded rocky compressions.

Remember the stronger the veining is stated in line, the softer it must be expressed in colour. Avoid hard brush strokes and continuous curving lines.

Paint Gouache colours in yellow ochre, raw sienna, raw umber, black and white, glycerine.

Equipment 10 cm (4 in) flat brush, soft cloth, polythene film, glaze containers, flat fitch, artists' brush.

Method Prepare a grey-yellow glaze by blending yellow ochre, black and white. Thin to transparency. Add a few drops of glycerine to reduce the drying time and apply to the ground with a medium flat brush. Immediately rag-off or rag-roll off using a loosely-bunched soft cloth. Identify the major veining elements by wiping out with a clean cloth or cotton bud. Allow to dry.

Prepare three semi-opaque glazes in different tones of the same colour by blending yellow ochre, raw sienna, black and white. Apply in loose, irregular patches with a cloth to produce a tonally textured effect.

Dab these areas with crumpled up polythene or a crisp cloth to produce a fractured veining pattern. Allow to dry.

Fidget in the main veins using the deepest tone thinned to transparency. Where the veins enter the toned areas emphasize the pattern created by the polythene by painting in fine lines with an artists' brush. Allow to dry. Strengthen accents with opaque paint.

Seal and protect with two coats of varnish.

Alternative technique

Paint Any pastel coloured gouache.

Equipment 10 cm (4 in) flat brush, soft cloth, newspaper.

Method Prepare a semi-transparent glaze in the chosen colour and apply with a brush to the ground.

Rag-roll off the applied glaze while wet using a softly gathered cloth. Fold a newspaper into sharp creases. Drop the newspaper onto the wet glaze and push it over the surface with a brush. Where the glaze comes in contact with the creases it is removed or displaced on the surface producing a plausible veining pattern.

LAMINATED MARBLE

Laminated marbles were produced when beds of limestone rock were crystallized into clearly defined layers, which remained largely undisturbed. When they were quarried and cut they revealed the stratified form. They are represented in paint as fine, roughly parallel, gently undulating bands of transparent colour superimposed on a pale ground. Although they occur naturally as greens, yellows, beiges and violets, fantasy finishes may be constructed in any softly stated pastel. Where panels are to be marbled the bands are depicted as slightly angled horizontals. Marbled columns exhibit a strong vertical accent.

A combination of the techniques of combing, stippling and wiping out are used in this simulation.

Paint A selected gouache colour. Glycerine.

Equipment Stippling brush, cotton bud, 10 cm (4 in) flat brush, home-made combs.

Method This technique involves building up laminated bands of colour over the entire panel using large combs approximately 23 cm (9 in) in length. These combs can be made from plastic squeegees or windscreen wiper blades.

First, prepare semi-transparent glazes in light, medium and dark tones from the selected colour. Add a few drops of glycerine to extend the drying time.

Using a large brush, apply a glaze in the darkest tone to the entire surface. Cut one of the combs to the required pattern (fig. 27) and pull through the wet glaze with a wavy motion. This has the effect of producing fine bands

27 *Apply the dark glaze to the prepared ground. Beginning at one edge, pull a 23 cm (9 in) comb cut from a plastic squeegee through the wet glaze using a slightly wavy motion. Repeat the process across the entire surface.*

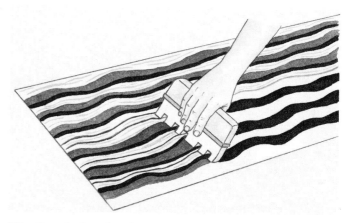

28 *Once the first glaze has dried, apply the mid-tone glaze and repeat the process with a second comb cut to a more detailed pattern. This produces the distinctive, fine, roughly undulating bands of transparent colour that are characteristic of the laminated marbles.*

of colour, for where the sponge touches the surface the glaze is removed to reveal the ground. Angling the comb will cause the bands to undulate.

Stipple the bands to soften the edges and allow to dry.

Apply the mid-tone glaze over the entire surface. Pull a combing tool, cut to a more detailed pattern, through the glaze, and stipple to soften the edges (fig. 28).

Apply the lightest glaze to the entire panel and using a cotton bud wipe out small irregular bands to reveal the ground. Finally create accents by applying opaque paint with an artists' brush. Leave to dry.

Seal and protect with two or three coats of varnish.

FOSSILIFEROUS MARBLES

These marbles exhibit the fossilized remains of small creatures entombed in the limestone strata many millions of years ago. They exist in a range of shapes and forms varying in size from about 2 cm (¾ in) to 10 cm (4 in). Their patterns are repeated throughout the marble and for this simulation many everyday objects can be used to print their variable forms. For example, a loofer cut lengthways or across its section leaves a print similar to the skeletal remains of a small fish; coiled rope and notched corks resemble shell forms; while all sorts of sliced vegetables can be used to represent sea creatures long extinct.

Paint Gouache colours in cobalt blue, black and white. Glycerine.

Equipment 10 cm (4 in) flat brush, soft cloth, paper, printing elements, talcum powder.

Method Prepare three tones of a blue-grey glaze by blending cobalt blue, black and white with water.

Thin the deepest tone to transparency, and add a few drops of washing up liquid to reduce the surface tension. Take up the glaze on the printing elements, and test the

29 *A fossilized marble*

effect they produce on paper before applying them to the ground. When you are happy with the results, randomly print over the ground. Do not worry if the prints are imperfect or blurred. Allow to dry.

With a transparent mid tone glaze rag-roll the entire surface. Press the dry printing elements onto the surface to remove the glaze. (Dry the elements regularly and dust them with talcum powder.) Arrange the prints in defined patches to suggest the route for a veining pattern.

When the second glaze is dry use a semi-opaque, white-blue glaze to print random fossils sparingly onto the surface.

Wipe out the veining pattern implied by the patches of fossil prints and fidget in the veins using a thinned glaze of the deepest tone.

Seal and protect with varnish.

5 MARBLING WITH OIL-BASED PAINTS

The specific marbles described in this chapter were selected as being representative of a vast range of coloured stones employed within the field of decoration. Mastery of the techniques employed in their simulation will provide a blue-print for systematically tackling any marble that may attract your attention or in fact any marble that may exist in your imagination. Although brief descriptions are provided for each marble, there can be no substitute for viewing the actual stone.

There are no hard and fast rules for capturing specific visual characteristics. With experience one is able to develop speed and assurance by identifying those techniques which best suit one's own abilities and requirements.

For the sake of practicability, the simulations in this chapter will be carried out on a 60 cm × 90 cm (2 in × 3 in) panel suitably prepared with a white eggshell ground (page 33). Wherever possible refer to a sample of the natural stone. Remember also to draft out a rough sketch of your design onto the panel. Although this will be concealed beneath paint, it allows an initial appreciation of the scale and disposition of line and colour within the design.

WHITE VEINED MARBLE

White veined marble has a cloudy, veiled white background against which are featured imprecise veining patterns in tones of grey. The surface is dotted with irregular patches of opaque white. Occasionally streaks of powder yellow or green are visible in the depths. They cross the ground without reference to the major veining patterns.

Paint Artists' oils in black, ultramarine, raw umber and yellow ochre. Undercoat, white spirit and scumble glaze.

Equipment Large flat brush, medium flat fitch, medium artists' brush, hogs hair softener.

Method Thin white undercoat one part paint to one part white spirit and apply to the prepared ground.

Arrange the colours in tonal order around the palette, and prepare a glaze of light and dark grey. For dark grey blend white undercoat, ultramarine and black; for light grey blend white undercoat with black and yellow ochre.

Fidget the light grey glaze onto the wet surface in small irregular patches using a medium fitch. Now repeat the procedure using the dark grey tone more sparingly in between the light grey areas. Blend and soften horizontally and vertically using the hogs hair softener.

For this marble the veins should be softly stated and are introduced onto the wet ground so that they too may be softened and blended. Thin the light grey tone with white spirit to achieve a greater transparency. Fidget the vein onto the ground with a shaking hand. Soften in the direction of the vein. Repeat the procedure for the darker tone of grey, but apply more sparingly. Allow the panel to dry.

Now prepare a thin white wash using undercoat and white spirit and apply it to the entire surface of the panel. Detail the opaque white irregular patches on the wet surface. Soften in all directions and allow to dry.

Finally, seal and protect the panel with two coats of polyurethane varnish.

Variations

Instead of using undercoat for the initial base coat, use white gloss mixed with white spirit and repeat the procedure. Gloss has certain protective qualities and therefore a coat of polyurethane varnish need not be applied. This is advantageous as varnish yellows with age and can reduce the effectiveness of the finish.

The veining pattern may be drawn in using black and grey oil-based crayons. The pattern is drawn in the wet ground and may be partially softened with a dry brush.

Apply a thin white gloss before the ground has set. In this case the opaque white patches may be produced by wiping out sections of glaze to expose the ground.

BLACK AND GOLD

This marble is popularly known as Portoro. It has a distinctive yellowy-gold chainlike veining pattern that is featured against a solid black ground clouded with a thin mist like cigarette smoke. The chain formations occur as vertical elements that run roughly parallel down the length of the panel; they converge and separate without ever touching having a maximum of about 20 cm (8 in) of ground between them.

Paint Black eggshell, artists' oils in white, raw umber, burnt sienna and chrome. Scumble glaze and white spirit.

Equipment 13 cm (5 in) flat brush, large sable brush, softener.

Method Prepare the ground by applying two thin coats of black eggshell to the panel. Allow to dry.

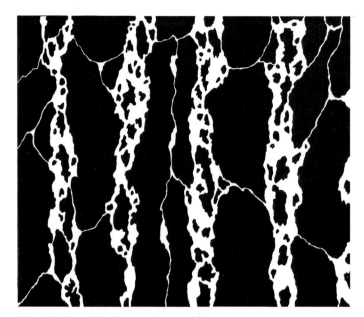

30 *Black and Gold*

Oil-in the ground sparingly by applying a thinned coat of scrumble glaze to the entire surface.

Prepare three tones of semi-opaque yellow glaze by blending chrome, burnt sienna and raw umber with white spirit.

Using an artists' brush well charged with the thinned scumble glaze take up two different tones of the prepared yellow glazes. Construct the veins by working in a continuous wavering motion down the panel. Rotate the brush and adjust the pressure on the bristles to vary the thickness, tone and intensity of line. Alternate the glazes to achieve continual changes within the veining pattern.

After the yellow veins have been applied, a cork or pencil eraser may be used to form the veins into more interesting shapes by displacing the paint on the wet surface.

Many people draw a halt at this stage believing that the clouding of the ground detracts from the purity and simplicity of the statement.

Prepare a thin grey wash by blending white and black with white spirit. Using a lightly charged medium flat fitch, apply the transparent white in the form of an imprecise, sketchy, diagonal veining pattern.

When the work is dry it is sealed with polyurethane varnish.

ST ANNES MARBLE

This marble is produced in the same way as Portoro. The background is satin black and the veins are depicted in tones of yellow. The pattern however is more uniformly distributed, has a diagonal slant, and is more intensely stated.

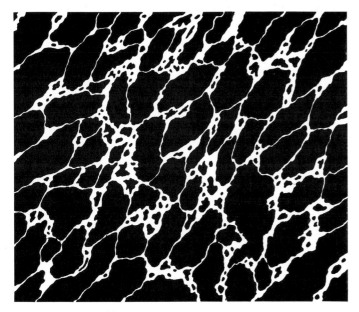

31 *St Annes marble*

ROUGE ROI

Rouge Roi is a red fossiliferous marble quarried in Belgium. It varies in colour from reddy-brown through to deep fawns. The red mottled ground is broken with white veins and patchy areas of bluey-grey and white.

Paint Artists' oils in Venetian red, Indian red, ochre, burnt sienna, ultramarine, black and white. Scumble glaze. White spirit.

Equipment Medium fitch, and artists' brush, hogs hair softener, clean cloth, paper, cork or pencil eraser.

Method Oil-in the ground by applying a thinned coat of scumble glaze to the entire panel.

Prepare a blue-grey glaze by blending ultramarine, black and white with white spirit. Apply in patches to the ground with a cloth. Mottle some areas by cissing with white spirit and then blending with a softener. Stipple other areas with a coarse sponge. Wipe out areas that are to be represented as fossils or veins using a cloth, or alternatively displace the paint with a cork or pencil eraser. Allow to dry.

Blend Venetian red and ochre with white spirit to produce a soft red glaze. Apply with a cloth to the ground, leaving the wiped out areas and a few patches of grey free of colour.

Prepare deeper tones of red by blending Indian red and black with white spirit. Also prepare a glaze of burnt sienna. Apply these glazes to the ground to strengthen and texture the existing red. Do not encroach however on the grey or white areas.

Break up the red areas by cissing: crumpled paper dipped first in a thin glaze of blue-black, then in white spirit is stippled on the surface. The glaze opens to reveal the ground producing a fractured appearance.

Strengthen the wiped out fossil shapes and major veins with dilute white. The entire ground is blended and softened.

Washes of blue-black are applied to tone down and harmonize the ground. Allow to dry. The surface is then protected and sealed with two coats of polyurethane varnish.

In this room, fantasy veined marbled wall panels have been framed by flat paint borders for emphasis. The table is a particularly good example of a serpentinuous marble, Vert de Mer.

ROJO ALICANTE

Rojo Alicante is a dramatic marble that features an extensive veining pattern. The background is predominantly yellow-red interspersed with sweeping ovals of grey-green. Superimposed in the foreground, the veins hang like torn white fabric floating in the breeze.

Paint Davies grey, burnt sienna, viridian, white spirit, scumble glaze.

Equipment Large sable brush, medium artists' brush, cloth and cotton buds.

Method Oil-in the ground by applying a thinned coat of scumble glaze to the entire ground.

Prepare a glaze of burnt sienna and a glaze of green-grey by blending a small amount of viridian and Davies grey with white spirit. Apply patches of light and dark burnt sienna uniformly over the ground with a cloth. Apply swirls of the grey-green glaze avoiding hard angles. Soften and blend. Allow to dry.

Apply a transparent glaze of grey-white to the entire ground and allow to dry.

The extensive veining pattern characteristic of this marble is produced by wiping out the glaze back to the ground. A large sable brush loaded with white spirit is used to ciss the glaze. Larger areas are removed with a cloth, fine sections with a cotton bud. The disposition of the veining pattern relates to the position on the background of the grey-green swirls. Emphasize detail with opaque colours.

Seal and protect with varnish.

RED LEVANTO

Strictly speaking Red Levanto is a serpentinious marble. Although it features randomly distributed patches of deep red, they are scattered over a green ground. The ground is broken by a sinewy white veining pattern that swirls round the angular red formations giving the impression of sea breaking on rocks. Larger white veins cross the foreground snaking around the red patches.

Paint Viridian, crimson lake, ultramarine, white, scumble glaze, white spirit.

Equipment Cloth, cork, pencil eraser mediun sable brush.

Method As an exception to the rule for marbling with oil paints, the ground is not oiled-in. Prepare a red-purple glaze by combining crimson lake, ultramarine and white spirit. Prepare a glaze of viridian. Blend these with an excess of scumble glaze and apply the glazes to the ground in patches. Refer to a drawing or sample to indicate the position of the larger areas of red-purple. The glazes will merge slightly. Allow to dry.

Prepare a transparent purple-grey wash by blending white with small quantities of ultramarine, crimson lake and viridian. Apply the glaze to all but the prominent red areas. Wipe out the glaze to emphasize the hard edges of the red sections. Wipe out to reveal smaller areas of green and red that may be seen beneath the glaze. Wipe out small areas back to the ground to reveal hard white.

To indicate the major veining pattern, ciss the ground using a medium sable brush loaded with white spirit. The glaze will open up to define their path. Paint in the minor veining pattern with an artists' brush using transparent white.

Develop these in patches over the ground linking the more colourful areas that have been wiped out. Strengthen features in opaque colour.

Apply thin washes of red and grey purple to harmonize the composition. Allow to dry. Seal and protect with varnish.

BOIS JOURDAN

Bois Jourdan is a beautiful marble that features loose irregular patches of deep red scattered carelessly over a grey-white mottled ground. The two elements are linked by a sparse veining pattern in yellow gold and grey. The veins are extremely convoluted and follow a tortuous route across the ground. Where the veins come in contact with the scattered red sections, both harden off to a sharp edge.

Paint Artists' oils in Paynes grey, burnt sienna, Indian red, yellow ochre, gold powder, scumble glaze, white spirit.

Equipment Fine artists' brush, crisp cloth or paper, cotton buds for wiping out.

Method Oil-in the ground by applying a thinned coat of scumble glaze with a cloth.

Prepare glazes of Paynes grey and burnt sienna by blending with white spirit. Thin to transparency and apply to the ground in patches. Ciss with white spirit and soften to produce undulating shady patches. Allow to dry out, but not completely.

Prepared a glaze of Indian red; thin with white spirit and a touch of scumble glaze, and apply with a crisp cloth, or paper, in patches to the surface. Overlap some of the darker areas beneath. The edges of the red patches will bleed onto nearly-dry glaze below to produce an imprecise, ragged effect.

Using a cotton bud dipped in white spirit, wipe-out patches of the glaze to indicate the passage of the veins. Prepare glazes of yellow ochre, grey and gold. Fidget in the veins in ochre and grey with a fine artists' brush. Create accents with gold and black.

Sometimes with this marble cloudy broad bands of white cross the foreground. These may be picked out with a broad sable brush loaded with a transparent white glaze.

Seal and protect the finished panel with two coats of varnish.

CIPOLLINO

Cipollino is an example of a laminated marble. Laminated marbles were formed when pressure and heat crystallized beds of limestone into roughly parallel bands. The marble is quarried and cut to reveal the strata which is generally exhibited in buildings as a vertical or horizontal accent.

The Cipollino variety is the name given to a group which features a white ground crossed by undulating bands of colour. The colours range from yellow through to grey and violet.

Paint raw sienna, Prussian blue, viridian, white spirit, scumble glaze.

Equipment Medium flat fitch, 5 cm (2 in) flat brush, medium artists' brush.

Method Prepare a grey-green glaze by blending raw sienna and Prussian blue with white spirit. Use this glaze to lightly tint sufficient scumble glaze to cover the prepared ground, and use this to oil-in the ground.

Prepare deeper tones of the grey-green by tinting with viridian. Sparingly apply bands of this glaze using the fitch. Between these bands of glazes leave a margin of the white ground showing which should appear clean and undulating.

Soften the bands in the direction of the strata and lightly stipple.

Seal and protect with a coat of varnish.

VERT DE MER

Vert de Mer is an example of the green marbles. Green marbles are characterized by the presence of the mineral serpentine. Although considerable variations occur in their structure, they are commonly identified by the striking tones of green that cloud the dark ground. The luminosity of the greens establishes an immediate sense of depth and translucency within the stone.

The green ground of Vert de Mer, which has a slight diagonal accent, is crossed by fine intermeshing veining patterns depicted in a lighter tone of green. The veins are uniformly distributed across the mid ground. The major veining patterns are white to grey and cross the foreground as intersecting diagonals.

Paint Black eggshell, artists' oils in Prussian blue, raw sienna, viridian green, white and black, scumble glaze, white spirit.

Equipment Feathers, 5 cm (2 in) flat brush and a medium artists' brush, cloth.

Method Prepare an eggshell ground in black in a similar manner to the procedure described on page 33.

Oil-in the ground by applying a coat of thinned scumble glaze, with a cloth to the dry ground.

Prepare a dark green glaze by blending raw sienna and Prussian blue with white spirit. Thin to transparency and using a feather dipped first in white spirit, then in the scumble glaze, take up the glaze and apply it loosely to the ground. Imply a slight diagonal; leave approximately a quarter of the ground showing and lightly ciss the glaze by spattering with white spirit. Leave to slightly harden off.

To form the secondary veining pattern of a fine intermeshing network, prepare a lighter green glaze by blending viridian and white with white spirit. Take a feather with the fronds broken into fine elements, charge with the glaze and construct the veins in transparent colour. Allow to dry.

The major veins are introduced in white as more positively stated intersecting diagonals. They cross the foreground close to the surface. These should be applied with an artists' brush.

Prepare a thin wash of dark yellow-green by adding a little black to the darker green glaze. Apply two or three washes to the surface to harmonize the colours. Seal and protect with two coats of varnish.

SIENNA

The name comes from the Italian province where the marble is quarried. It is variegated marble that exhibits

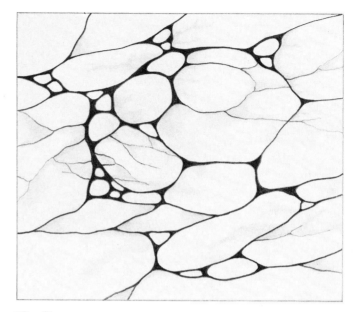

32 *Sienna*

great variations in colour and translucency ranging from light creams through yellows to reds. The veining patterns vary from fine intermeshing systems in white and grey to the more powerfully stated, dramatic elements in reds, blacks and purples. The veins enclose irregular pebble shapes, the smaller increments clinging to the major veins like stones on a necklace.

Paint Artists' oils in raw sienna, burnt sienna, chrome, Indian red and ultramarine blue, scumble glaze, white spirit.

Equipment Four 2.5 cm (1 in) brushes (one for each glaze), cloth, hogs hair softener, artists' brush, paper.

Method Oil-in the ground by applying thinned scumble glaze with a brush or cloth.

Prepare glazes of burnt sienna, chrome, raw sienna and grey-violet. Grey-violet is produced by combining Indian red and ultramarine with white spirit. Using separate brushes for each glaze, dip the brush first in white spirit and then in scumble glaze before taking up the glaze and applying it to the surface. Refer to a sample or sketch of the natural stone to determine the position of the darker glazes. Soften and blend the patches of colour together.

Ciss the surface by stippling the wet glazes with a screwed up piece of paper moistened with white spirit. Where smaller shapes are to be identified, introduce spots of solvent into the glaze by means of a brush. Soften in all directions.

Texture the ground by applying loose washes of white grey and yellow. This has a cohesive effect and neutralizes some of the more strident colours. Soften once more.

Reinforce the natural patterns produced in the cissing process by introducing veins. The veins will be drawn around large and small oval shapes.

On a palette produce a reddy-brown glaze by blending Indian red and burnt sienna with white spirit. Small quantities of ultramarine are now added to tone down the glaze to a grey-purple. Ultramarine and Indian red are blended with white spirit to produce a violet-grey. These colours of grey-purple and violet-grey are used to produce the major veining patterns. Either load the two glazes onto one brush or use separate brushes.

The secondary veins encompass the larger shapes and link them to the major veins. They are more softly stated in colour and transparency. Blend raw and burnt sienna with white spirit and scumble glaze to produce reddy-yellow browns. Again, use the cissed pattern to identify the course of the vein applying the colour with a fine artists' pencil. At this stage some of the smaller oval shapes are wiped-out to reveal the ground to introduce highlights. The larger veins are strengthened using a fine brush.

After allowing the work to dry the ground is toned down by applying washes of the colours already used.

This will have the effect of harmonizing your marbled panel. Allow to dry.

The finish is sealed and protected with two coats of mid sheen polyurethane varnish.

BRECHE VIOLET

This marble is quarried in the Carrara mountains in Italy. It has great popular appeal because of its forthright, honest patterning and clean translucent colour. The busy fragmented sections are often featured as stratified layers contrasted against anonymous backgrounds of pale cloudy marble.

Paint Artists' oils in white, crimson lake, ochre, black, ultramarine, scumble glaze, white spirit.

Equipment Cloth, medium flat fitch, hogs hair softener, medium artists' brush.

Method Oil-in the ground. Apply the scumble glaze to the ground using a brush or cloth.

Produce a grey-pink glaze by blending white, crimson lake and ochre with white spirit. Produce a grey-violet glaze by blending white, black and ultramarine. Thin them to transparency and apply them in random patches to the ground using a cloth.

Prepare deeper tones of the reds, purples and violet-greys by blending crimson lake, ultramarine, black and white. Apply the glazes to those areas that are to be more heavily veined.

Soften and blend the ground.

Major veins are represented in varying strengths of line and tone in grey-violet using an artists' brush. Secondary veins should be more softly stated in tones of the reddish-violet glaze.

Areas enclosed by veins that are too powerfully stated are neutralized by applying thin washes of white and grey. Emphasize some veins by applying opaque white with an artists' brush. Opaque white areas are also introduced to some of the smaller enclosed stones by

This bath and hand-basin have been encased in a marbled unit exhibiting a fossilized Sienna marble type.

painting in or wiping out. These proliferate around the intersections of major veins. The surface is now allowed to dry out.

Several washes of grey-violet are applied to the dried surface to tone down the prominent colour and harmonize the ground.

The work is allowed to dry and is then sealed and protected with polyurethane varnish.

6   MARBLING IN THE HOME

This section is included to guide and hopefully inspire those who have gained a certain mastery of the techniques but are unsure where they might most satisfactorily be employed within the home.

CORRIDORS, HALLWAYS AND STAIRS

The home is divided up into rooms where we eat, sleep, cook, bathe and relax, linked by corridors, stairwells, landings and halls. Because they are difficult to incorporate in design schemes these areas are often neglected, becoming dowdy and anonymous. A marbled theme here will help to re-vitalize these areas and will establish continuity and character throughout.

A marbled floor design constructed on the diagonal will always imply movement and flow. It is compelling without being obtrusive. Lay it throughout these linking areas. Vary pattern or colour if you feel it is becoming monotonous or strident. Black on white is always a safe bet, however don't be harnessed by convention.

Alternatively, establish continuity between these linking areas by marbling the wall surfaces. Remember these areas tend to be rather confined spaces; distance the walls by using translucent pale colours. Where the stairwell passes from one floor to the next accentuate the link by emphasizing the vertical element in the veining pattern. But do not waste time on unnecessary detail as people tend to move quickly through rather than dwell in these areas. Use a quick drying water-based marble technique.

DOORS

These soulless surfaces can be turned into *object d'art*. Feature marbled panels by contrasting them against raised areas which have been painted in an opaque colour or with a complementary marble technique. Or increase the visual strength of the door by incorporating the door frame in the technique. Even items as small as the door knobs or handles can receive detailed treatment by spattering techniques.

Often the most practical way to marble the door is simply to take it off its hinges. This will allow the work to be tackled on a horizontal plane, causing a minimum of fuss and inconvenience.

LIVING ROOM

The living room is perhaps the most important room in the house. A communal room for relaxation, and for entertaining friends and acquaintances. A marbled theme here cannot fail to impress. If large areas such as the walls are to be marbled, they must be softly stated in line and colour. Keep heavy patterns and colours below dado height, as placed above a lighter element they will make the room top heavy. Floors may receive a bolder treatment, but remember to plan your design around large items of furniture, otherwise your hard work will be hidden from view.

Traditional applications in the living room usually involve marbling the fireplace, skirting boards, picture and dado rails with one technique. Fireplaces especially are a popular choice. White veined marble is usually selected, but try a breche or laminated marble as an alternative. Or introduce a colourful fantasy technique theme with a strong random pattern that offsets the strict geometry of the piece. Apply it sparingly and contrast it against a softly stated yellowy-green ground.

Try marbling items of furniture in the room, for example, the table. Small table tops divided into geometric sections, each given its own individual detailed treatments can look exquisite without being overbearing. Gilt or mirror inlay can amplify the effect. Tables of more generous proportions can be given dramatic treatments to convert them into monumental slabs. Remember to continue your treatment over the edge to imply thickness. Glass tables provide a wonderful surface on which to marble, and these can be backlit to increase luminosity.

BATHROOM
In the bathroom traditionally the skirting board and bath surround are marbled. However, in view of the tremendous empathy that water and marble have for each other, virtually every surface in the room can be marbled as long as the overall effect is kept light and airy.

The bathroom suite provides a natural foil or contrast and colours should be carefully chosen to incorporate these within the theme. Alternatively, why not marble the bathroom suite? But remember to apply a coat of ceramic paint to seal the surface before beginning. And remember to protect finished marbled surfaces from moisture by sealing with polyurethane varnish.

KITCHENS
Kitchens tend to be full of noise, colour and confusion. Work surfaces and wall areas at eye level are best kept free of all but the most unobtrusive geometric patterning. There would seem little point in constructing a marbled theme that had to compete with soap powder packets, food blenders and gaudy-handled kitchen utensils.

However, cupboards situated high up or low down can be considered. Melamine surfaces, provided they are lightly abraded, provide excellent surfaces on which to marble. Doors on kitchen units may be removed, marbled on the horizontal, and replaced with the minimum amount of disruption.

If you should decide to tackle the fridge, cooker or washing machine, remember that they will be out of use for a few days. And should you decide on a marbled floor, remember it is a heavily-used surface and must be protected with several coats of polyurethane varnish.

BEDROOMS
Traditionally a marbled theme in the bedroom incorporates the skirting board and the wall against which the bed head rests. But why not try a more imaginative approach in this most private of rooms.

Remember for much of the time the bedroom will be artificially lit. Reflective foils and precious shells can produce a magical, starlit, back-drop incorporated into a black and gold fossilized marble; or use gold veining chains against a satin white ground.

A marbled floor in the bedroom may be wasted as the bed takes up a great deal of room. But why not marble the ceiling instead? Centre your design around the ceiling rose. (Ceilings tend to be unobtrusive, so be adventurous with your selection of pattern and colour.) Draw up onto graph paper and transfer the dimensions to a plastic film such as Fablon. Marble onto the Fablon, cut out the required sections and stick them on the ceiling. Be careful to refer the sections accurately to the graph paper plan, as Fablon is powerfully adhesive and difficult to readjust once in position.

Another idea is to marble the bedhead and bedside furniture. Use an exotic colour such as black or deep purple, and feature small reflective items.

CONSERVATORY AND EXTENSION

Glazed surfaces provide an excellent opportunity to show off the beauty of transparent colour. Although oil- or water-based paint may be used, specially-formulated colours are available from artists' shops for use on glass. The colours cannot be blended, but constructed as a stained glass window, marbled themes are always well received. Position high up so they may be viewed against the sky.

Or construct a classical theme amongst the greenery. A whole range of decorative pots and statuettes are available from DIY or garden centres at a nominal price. Suitably prepared, marbled and positioned on a white marble floor they can evoke a serene atmosphere.

If protected with several coats of polyurethane varnish all these marbled objects can be displayed out of doors to extend the classical theme to your garden. Build the ruins of a classical Greek temple or obelisk from polyurethane foam and plastic drain-piping. Both materials are easily sawn, prepared and marbled and provide excellent props for this type of situation. Marbled ornamental pools and fountains are only refinements of simple techniques.

7 APPLICATIONS

WALLS

Walls are the most important decorative feature within a room; their surfaces carry the largest areas of colour and are primarily responsible for the creation of atmosphere mood and style.

Although their prominence affords us an ideal opportunity to exploit the full illusory potential of the marbling technique, we must remember that wall surfaces are subject to close scrutiny; good paint practice is vital if we are to obtain a credible simulation.

Preparation of wall surfaces

As much of the wall surface is at eye level every effort should be made to ensure the prepared ground is of a high standard. Remember paint can neither flatten ripples or bridge cracks.

Painted surfaces If the surface is in good order it will need only to be washed with hot water and detergent. Glossed surfaces, however, should be lightly sanded to provide a key for the ground coat.

Flaking surfaces should be sanded to remove loose paint, repaired if necessary with a filler, and then sealed with a proprietory paint sealer.

Wallpapered surfaces If the paper is in good order and does not carry an embossed pattern, it will provide a suitable surface for a ground coat to be applied to. (Washable wallpapers are not suitable for the application of an emulsion ground coat.) Wipe the paper down sparingly with hot water and detergent.

Surfaces that are unsound should be stripped. Care should be taken not to gouge the underlying plaster. Wallpaper stripping machines are available on hire from most decorating shops. Alternatively, use plenty of hot water and elbow grease.

Plaster surfaces Sound plaster surfaces need only be washed with hot water and detergent. Plaster surfaces that have aged or cracked, however, should be filled. Shallow indentations should be lightly abraded and relieved before applying a proprietory filler. The filler should be mixed to a runny paste and applied with a paintbrush. When hard, the surface should be sanded flat using medium grade sandpaper mounted on a rubbing block. For large cracks repeat the operation using the filler as a stiff paste.

If the surface contains a great many imperfections, it should be covered with lining paper and a coat of size applied to the surface before the application of paint. Size is a medium which is used to seal the surface.

Designing a panel system

Take accurate measurements of the area to be marbled and draw up the dimensions of the area onto graph paper. Remember to indicate the positions of such visual accents as dados, picture rails, friezes and skirting boards. These elements were traditionally incorporated and positioned within rooms to create harmonious

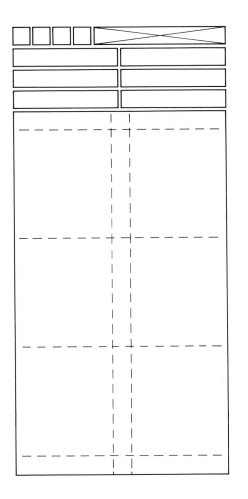

33 *Marking out a 240 × 120 cm (8 × 4 ft) sheet of hardboard to produce a well-proportioned, harmonious wall panel. By careful planning it is possible to avoid waste.* **Left** *The required design is scaled up from graph paper onto the panel. The small sections are carefully cut out and saved, and the dotted lines are emphasized to indicate individual panels that are to be marbled. The crossed section is the only redundant piece.* **Right** *The smaller sections are marbled in a contrasting technique and are then positioned around the marbled panel to form a border*

proportions and can provide useful guidelines when marbling a wall. However do not be dominated by them. If they cannot be removed, more often than not they can be camouflaged.

Overlay the graph paper with tracing paper and draw up the required design. If large areas are to be marbled, remember they must be broken down into smaller components or panels so that manageable sections can be tackled.

Take measurements from your design, scale up to normal size and reconstruct them on the prepared wall surface using tape measure, plumb line, spirit level and straight edge. Blue chalk can be used as a marker; it will dissolve beneath the applied glazes.

Panel shapes may be emphasized by constructing a border in a contrasting marbling theme or contrasting the panel against a flat paint finish.

Panelling system using hardboard

Rather than marbling directly onto the wall surface the technique can be worked on to sheets of hardboard. The advantages of using hardboard panels are (a) the room is only out of action for as long as it takes to mount the completed boards, (b) when it comes to change the decor, the panels can be taken down and put up elsewhere in the house, (c) irretrievably damaged wall surfaces are concealed, and (d) marbling can take place on the horizontal.

Buy 240 × 120 cm (8 ft × 4 ft) sheets of hardboard, 4 mm (1/8 in) thick.

If a hardboard system is to be used these dimensions should be given due consideration in designing the scheme. While it is possible to represent each panel as a prepared board, fixing them to the surface can become tedious. Working on larger areas represents a more practical approach. Fig. 34 shows the possibilities for the economic use of the board.

Once you have drawn up a design for the panelled areas, the hardboard can be cut to the required dimensions; it is readily sawn but should be adequately supported during the process. Mark out your design and marble onto the shiny side of the board to carry out your technique. If water-based paints are to be used, the surface must be sealed with a proprietory sealer; oil-based paints can be applied directly to the surface.

When the panel is finished it should be placed in the room where it is to be hung for a couple of days. Shrinkage or expansion will take place as it acclimatizes to the room conditions.

Accurately mount the panel referring to guidelines using plumbline and spirit level. Secure the panels using rawlplugs and wood screws.

FLOORS

Floors provide a less critical surface than wall areas and can absorb a much greater saturation of colour and pattern. The floor creates the natural visual base of a room and should be several tones deeper in colour than the ceiling. If the reverse applies, the room can be disorientating and uncomfortable. Because the floor is not subjected to the same degree of scrutiny as the wall surfaces, preparation and finish can be more relaxed.

Preparation of floor surfaces

Wooden floorboards in good condition exhibit a strong visual accent. To correct this the gaps between the boards can be filled with a proprietory vinyl based seam filler. Natural wood will require sealing; painted boards need only be scrubbed with hot soapy water and allowed to dry. Both will require undercoating.

Wooden floorboards in poor condition must first be secured and then sanded using a light industrial tool. It is a messy business and is really a job for professionals. Heavily-varnished boards may require industrial strip-

A casual marbled theme can help to establish continuity and character throughout linking areas in the home, such as corridors, hallways, staircases and landings.

ping, in which case they will require deep sanding to remove char marks. The boards must then be filled, sanded, primed and undercoated. A good case for using hardboard panels?

Ceramic tiles These present much the same problem as floorboards in exhibiting strong visual accents and the joints should be filled in as above. Scrub with hot soapy water, allow to dry, and then undercoat.

Linoleum sheet or tiles provided they are in good order and carry no pattern relief, are suitable surfaces for marbling. Clean with hot soapy water, allow to dry and undercoat.

Designing a panel system
Traditionally marble floor designs are based around the strict geometry of a simple panelling system. The scale of individual panels to the total floor area is governed by the size of the room, for example, very large panels look incongruous in a small room, while an intricate pattern in a large room can become overbearing and fussy.

Large rooms benefit from formal rectilinear patterns using panels of colour which are tonally quite close. This will produce a static, tranquil atmosphere. Small rooms or spaces require greater contrasts and benefit from the use of a prominent diagonal accent. This produces an illusion of movement and causes the eye to travel over, rather than dwell or focus, on any particular spot. Anonymous rooms or spaces, often with several entrances, can be visually strengthened by constructing a feature or focal point in the floor design.

Before working out the floor design, take accurate measurements of the area to be marbled: rooms are seldom truly square, so measure the diagonals to ensure accuracy.

Draw up the plan on graph paper, and incorporate the positions of the fireplace, doors and windows. Use overlays of tracing paper to indicate the positions of

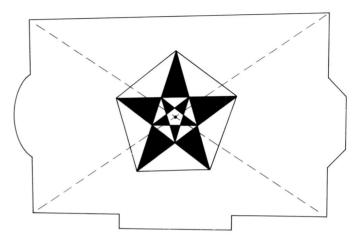

34 *A floor design should always generate from the centre point of a room. To find the centre point, measure the diagonals.*

permanent and movable items of furniture. This information will affect your design for there would be little point in hiding a decorative floor under large items of furniture.

The range of designs are endless, the limitation is merely one of imagination and commitment. As a variation on the traditional squared design, investigate possibilities generated by three and five sided figures or even circles or ellipses. If you wish to create a focal point in the centre of the room, the intersection of the diagonal should be used as the generating point for the design.

The prominent lines created by floorboards can be problematic. Although it is possible by diligent preparation to fill the joints between boards, it is difficult to completely lose the visual accent. Accentuating the cross pattern in your design, however, can distract the eye from this.

Rooms of course are seldom square-sided. Construct a border around the outer perimeter of your design to absorb the dimensional irregularities of the room. Work this border in a flat contrasting colour, or a marble

Marbled floor panels can be arranged in a wide variety of ways

35 *A static traditional square design is particularly suitable for a large room*

36 *A busy, moving diagonal design can be used in a small room to create a feeling of space*

37 *A triangle design*

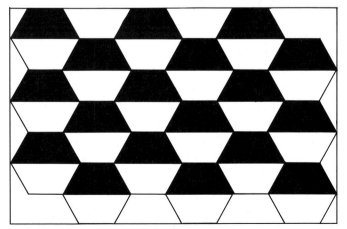

38 *The triangle design can be adapted to create an interesting hexagonal design*

Fantasy marbled squares have been used in combination with a flat paint finish to create a bold geometric design on this wooden floor.

simulation using a tight repetitive pattern, e.g. porphyry.

When you have mapped out a satisfactory design onto the graph paper floor plan, scale up the dimensions to normal size, and draw out the design onto a prepared floor surface. Always work out from the intersection of the diagonal.

When marbling directly onto a floor surface it is important to adopt a systematic approach. Do not paint yourself into a corner, always work towards the door.

Apply a ground coat (page 33) to a prepared surface and allow to dry for at least two days.

Once marbled the floor will require the protection of many layers of varnish, and the room will be out of use for some days.

Panelling system using hardboard
Using a hardboard panelling system to marble a floor has many advantages. Imperfections that might prove costly or time consuming to rectify or disguise are covered, as are distracting visual accents such as floorboards or ceramic tile patterning. Panels can be marbled and varnished off site and so the room is only out of use for as long as it takes to fix the panels.

High density 8 mm (¼ in) hardboard should be used. If greater structural integrity is required, one of the more substantial composites can be used such as chipboard, blockboard or plywood, but even when using oil-based paints these surfaces must be sealed before use.

Wherever possible use large areas of hardboard (240 cm × 120 cm; 8 in × 4 in sheets); breaking up sheets into the size of individual panels is unnecessary. If possible fix the panel through to the joist using counter-sunk cup washers and wood screws. The position of joists can be indicated on your floor plan.

By scaling down the hardboard sheets, use a tracing paper overlay to show the most economical way of using the board on your floor plan. If your design incorporates

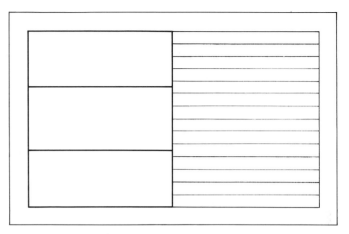

39   *The distracting geometry of floorboards can be camouflaged by laying marbled hardboard panels*

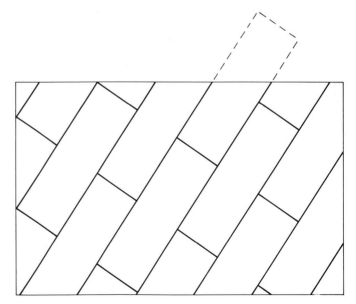

40   *By careful planning of your floor design, optimum use of hardboard panels can be achieved. The dotted section may be used as an infill section where an incomplete panel is required.*

a diagonal, reflect this in the direction you position the long edge of the board.

ARTEFACTS AND FURNITURE

Traditionally marbling techniques are applied to such items as fireplaces, table tops, large items of furniture and small ornaments. But any object can be marbled so long as it has a reasonably smooth surface without too much relief, and that this surface is capable of receiving paint.

The plastics industry for example produces an enormous range of products which carry smooth hard surfaces ideally suited for marbling, and a wide range of fibre-glass objects are available from garden centres and DIY shops, from garden furniture to statues, from columns to water fonts. Try out the technique on smooth stones or rocks and glass objects such as milk bottles, double-eyed drinking vessels, and goldfish bowls.

Small items can receive coloured treatments with strong vibrant patterns without competing with other painted surfaces in the room. Larger objects such as fireplaces or substantial items of furniture, a chest of drawers for example, must be treated in a more reserved fashion. Bold treatments can often result in the piece becoming monumental and overbearing.

Preparation of surfaces

Glass should be washed with hot soapy water to remove all traces of oil or grease. It should then be thoroughly dried and allowed to stand in a warm, dry atmosphere before priming with undercoat.

Metal surfaces in good order should be treated as above. If small areas of rust are evident, remove paint from the surrounding area. Remove some, but not all, the rust scale; apply a proprietory rust inhibitor and leave for a day before priming with undercoat. If the piece is severely rusted, it should be shot blasted, primed with a proprietory metal primer and then undercoated.

Plastic objects should be washed in hot soapy water using a scouring sponge. This will abrade the surface sufficiently for paint to grip to it. Allow to dry, and apply undercoat.

Fibre-glass surfaces vary enormously. Smooth flat surfaces should be lightly abraded with medium-dry glass paper to remove prominent nibbs or imperfections. Remove dust and prime with undercoat. Rough surfaces or surfaces covered with tiny pinholes should be thoroughly sanded with medium-grade glass paper, the dust removed and then painted with a proprietory fine grade filler thinned to the consistency of a paste. Allow to dry out completely before sanding with fine grade glass paper. Remove dust and apply an undercoat. Local repairs can be carried out in the same manner.

Painted wood in good condition should be washed with hot soapy water using a scouring sponge. Allow to dry and then apply an undercoat. Flaking paint can be treated as a local repair by sanding back and then priming.

Painted surfaces in poor condition must be stripped using a blow lamp or a proprietory paint stripper. If a paint stripper is used the surface must be scrubbed with water to remove all traces of it, and then allowed to dry. Sand and prime the stripped surface. Apply an undercoat.

Natural wood requires priming and undercoating. Polished natural wood should be cleaned using a fine grade wire wool and methylated spirits. The piece should be primed and undercoated.

8   FANTASY THEMES

FANTASY APPLICATIONS

This chapter aims to indicate the unexplored world that exists outside the conventional boundaries of traditional marbling. While within the limited scope of the text it is impossible to go into specific detail, it is hoped that the topics raised on the next few pages will serve as a source of inspiration for enthusiasts to go on to create their own marbled fantasies.

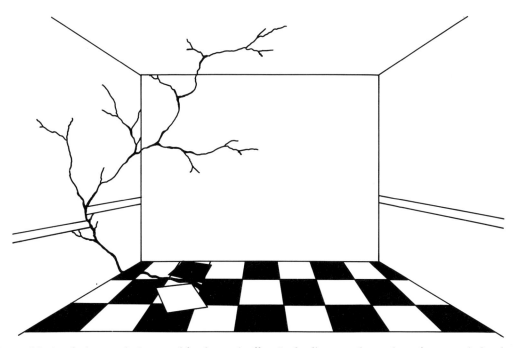

41   *The scale of a marble simulation can be increased for dramatic effect. In the diagram above a large fracture vein has been marbled across the ceiling, down the walls and across the floor, displacing the dado rail and the floor tiles.*

On a large scale

Increase the scale of your marble simulation by filling a wall, bridging a corner, and even linking wall, floor and ceiling to break up the rigid geometry of a room. As a powerfully stated design, large fracture veins travelling over a troubled ground can be very dramatic (fig. 41, page 69). As a softer theme, imprecise clouds and soft colour gradations can imply space and distance.

At first the idea of tackling such a theme may appear daunting. In fact it is merely an extension of the panel method; the design is broken down into sections that may be tackled comfortably in a few hours.

Select your marble sample or fantasy sketch and draw up on graph paper. Scale up your drawing and using lining paper or similar cut out the major elements within your design and position them on the surface to capture the general effect. Break the design down into manageable areas and proceed as normal with the simulation.

Crumbling opulence

Enclose some of your marbled theme within a jagged boundary to suggest a marble veneer that may have broken away from the wall exposing the brickwork beneath. Possibly one of the bricks is missing and a glimpse of a world beyond is suggested. The brickwork is, of course painted. Beneath the fractured panel, paint

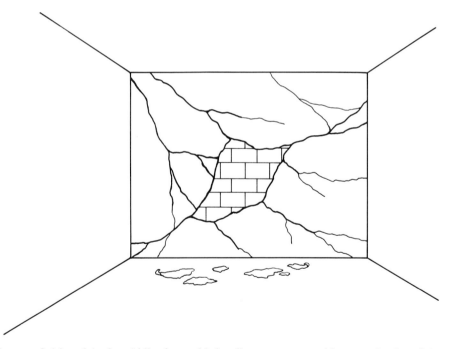

42 *Paint some brickwork in the middle of a marbled wall to suggest a marble veneer that has disintegrated with age*

scattered marbled fragments onto a marbled floor.

Or marble the fireplace, strip the room of all but the barest furniture, hang some torn drapes and you are immediately transported to the past grandeur of an Italian apartment or a French villa. To emphasise the effect create a Palladio floor.

A classical theme

A trompe l'oeil classical scene is always a source of amusement and delight. It has the added advantage of spacing out a cramped room or relieving a tight corner. The scene may depict a receding marbled corridor flanked by columns or statues with a marbled floor (possibly a continuation of the one in the room); or even a Roman baths.

Because of the strict geometric proportions of classical architecture, designs are easily constructed onto graph paper, scaled up and re-drafted onto the wall (fig. 43 and 44). Work your chosen marbling techniques in clearly defined areas like painting by numbers.

Columns are elements which feature strongly in all classical themes. While decorative columns may be bought from suppliers, they are expensive and costly to install. As a cheap alternative, plastic piping is available in a range of sizes; it may be combined with jointing accessories and attachments to produce an acceptable column. The material is easily cut with a hacksaw and its surface provides an excellent ground on which to marble. Combining various pipes can produce larger columns with a fluted appearance. Use columns to visually strengthen a door or window opening, or to define a space around a bed or in the garden.

An alternative method of making a column is to bend flexible plastic sheeting around circular formers and nail or staple into position.

Classical statues have great presence with their elegant poses and distant sad gazes. Always keep your eyes open for possible candidates; antique markets and garden centres are good hunting grounds. Remember the flatter their surfaces the less preparation will be required.

The most effective twentieth-century equivalent to the classical statue is the manikin. They are available for a nominal sum and have excellent surfaces for marbling. Do not marble the whole surface, possibly combine two or three techniques allowing the patterns to entwine the limbs.

Recent classics

Always keep your eyes open for small artefacts that are casualties of the disposable society. Often they have great character and presence and can be given a new lease of life with a sensitively applied deocrative theme.

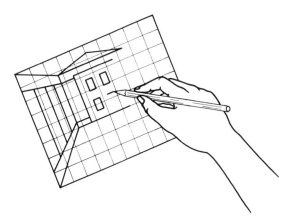

43 *Designing a trompe l'oeil classical scene on graph paper*

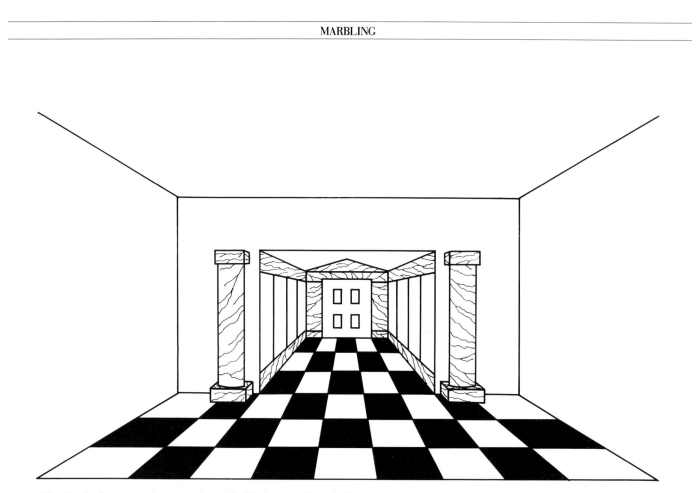

44 *Re-draft your design onto the wall. Work a marble technique on the painted columns either side of the door at the end of the trompe l'oeil corridor. Frame your design by constructing two columns from polystyrene blocks and marble them with a complementary technique.*

Some suitable objects might include telephones (especially if they are of the old hook variety), typewriters, guitars, or even a car wing displayed on a wall (retain the headlamp and winker and wire them up for an unusual wall lamp).

FANTASY FINISHES

Cracklure finishes

Cracklure materials are used to artificially antique or age a surface by simulating the natural degradation of highly-polished or lacquered finishes. They are marketed as a two pack system with comprehensive instructions. A slow drying oil-based varnish is first applied to a surface; while the surface is still tacky, a water-based varnish is applied. This coat dries quickly, shrinks, and in doing so produces a fine crazed pattern over the surface. Although the materials are supplied as transparent varnishes, they may be tinted with artists' oils and gouache colours respectively.

Icing on the cake

As a delicious foil to the glassy finish of a highly-polished marbling technique, try frosting part of the simulation. The process involves scattering sugar or salt in the final coat of varnish applied to the simulation. To get an idea of the effect place a piece of glass or perspex over your work; varnish the surface and apply the salt or sugar. Allow the varnish to dry out and wash off the excess sugar or salt with water. Place the glass over your simulation, and if you like what you see proceed with the process on your simulation. The surface will take on a frosted texture, looking and feeling like unpolished rock.

An alternative method of applying highlights to a finish is to scatter reflective foil or glitter elements into the final coats of varnish. Rather than scattering randomly, apply them to small areas or channels to suggest veining

routes. They disappear in daylight; in artificial light they twinkle like distant stars.

In a more relaxed vein

Veining is the most dramatic feature in marbling; below are listed a few cheerful fantasy ideas.

Method 1 Using a torn net curtain, preferably with thick strands and wide openings, stretch it over your surface. Distort the pattern and secure (fig. 45). Mask out areas of the ground to provide contrast. Using two or three aerosol cans available from car accessory shops,

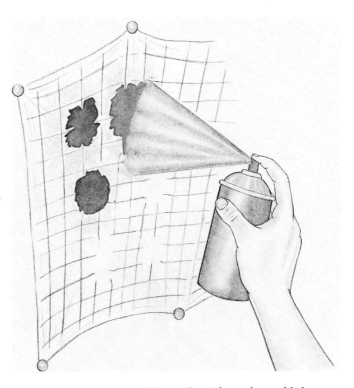

45 *Stretch a torn net curtain over the surface to be marbled. Distort the pattern to get the effect you want, and secure with pins. Spray randomly with an aerosol can.*

The shelves of this unusually designed drinks' trolley have been worked with a fossilstone marbling technique.

shake the canister well before appling random patches of colour to the ground. Allow to dry and remove the netting. Strengthen parts of the veining pattern using crayons or charcoal.

Method 2 Draw a jagged veining line on a piece of card. Cut the card into two sections along the line. Lay one half of the section on your prepared surface and using a well shaken aerosol apply paint in a fanning action fading out as you move further away from the cut out section. Remove the card. Using the other card section, lay it on the surface so that a gap exists between the hard edge of the painted vein and the section. Using a different colour, again fade out. Where the paints overlap, a vein will be produced. Repeat the process using the card sections over selected areas of the surface.

Method 3 Select a piece of hemp rope or similar, about 25 cm (10 in) in length and 4 mm (⅛ in)· in diameter. Unravel the strands to produce thick and thin sections that terminate in uneven ragged mops. Lay the rope on a flat surface and using a 7.5 cm (3 in) brush apply a coat of quick-drying white polish. Keep the strands flat and arrange the sections into veining patterns before the varnish hardens. Two or three coats will be adequate.

Using the stiffened rope as a stencil, lay it on your prepared surface and spray aerosol paint around it to leave a veining pattern. Repeat the process over the ground using different colours.

Method 4 Using paper for your technique, screw it up into a ball and spray the outside with different colours. Unfold the paper and iron out the creases.

Reflections
Marbling onto mirrors can produce some amazing effects. Apply a ground coat of white eggshell. Oil- or water-based marbling techniques may now be applied. When the simulation has dried, wipe out veining patterns

or rocky angular fragments. The effect can be featured by carefully positioning artificial light so that it is reflected from the wiped out sections. A sharp blade may be necessary to cut through the white eggshell base if it has been applied too thickly. Varnish.

FOSSILSTONE MARBLING
(Water-based paints)
In this technique we take advantage of the incompatibility of water-based paints and methylated spirits. Gouache colours applied over an oil-based ground of eggshell are cissed with methylated spirits, an alcohol-based solvent. Although little control may be exercised over the final disposition of colour, the technique is quick and the results charming. The surface exhibits a random distribution of small pools of transparent colour, each pool is ringed by transitions of deeper tonal hues.

This technique is best carried out on a horizontal surface.

Paint Three or four gouache colours, washing up liquid, methylated spririts.

Equipment 7.5 cm (3 in) flat brush, medium artists' brush, cotton buds, cloth.

Method Blend the gouache colours together to produce the required hue. Add a few drops of washing up liquid to lower the surface tension of the paint so that cissing may more readily take place.

Thin the glaze to a milky consistency and apply with the flat brush to the entire surface. Working quickly, ciss the paint by either spattering or running an artists' brush loaded with methylated spirits through the glaze.

As an addition, when dry, the surface may be wiped out to reveal fossil shapes or a veining pattern. Use cotton buds.

Using a mid tone glaze fidget in the veining pattern with a fine brush.

Seal and protect with varnish.

FOSSILSTONE MARBLING
(Oil-based paints)

Although finishes are similar to those produced in the water-based system, working in oils allows a much greater freedom and control in manipulating the surface.

Cissing agents ranging from methylated spirits, white spirit, turpentine and even water may be applied using all manner of tools; from feathers to eye droppers, from stiff bristled brushes to crumpled newspaper. The system offers a vast range of finishes and the only advice that can be given is let the solvent do the work; the skill lies in knowing when to stop.

Paint White spirit, turpentine, methylated spirits, artists' oils in three subdued earth colours.

Equipment 7.5 cm (3 in) flat brush, eye dropper, feathers, newspaper, cotton buds and a long-handled stencil brush.

Method Thin transparent oil glaze medium with white spirit and tint using the selected artists' oil colour. Apply generously to the surface using a flat brush.

Prepare glazes from the chosen colours by blending with white spirit. Dipping the brush first in white spirit and then in the medium, take up colour and apply to the surface in a checker board fashion. Repeat using the other glazes.

Sponge stipple to blend and overlap the colours.

To ciss use a crumpled newspaper dipped in white spirit to randomly dab the wet surface. Alternatively, release droplets of the solvent by banging the shaft of a loaded brush on a hard edge. Produce more transparent pools and cloudy effects by cissing with turpentine. Where the surface appears short of colour, introduce small circular patches of glaze from an eye dropper.

Seal and protect with varnish.

INDEX